DOUGLAS BADER

An Inspiration in Photographs

DOUGLAS BADER

An Inspiration in Photographs

Dilip Sarkar

Ramrod Publications

Dedication

This book is dedicated to amputees all over the world.

Other books by Dilip Sarkar:-

SPITFIRE SQUADRON: *19 Squadron at War, 1939-41*
THE INVISIBLE THREAD: *A Spitfire's Tale*
THROUGH PERIL TO THE STARS
ANGRIFF WESTLAND
A FEW OF THE MANY: *A Kaleidoscope of Memories*
BADER'S TANGMERE SPITFIRES: *The Untold Story, 1941*
BADER'S DUXFORD FIGHTERS: *The Big Wing Controversy*
MISSING IN ACTION: *Resting in Peace?*
GUARDS VC: *Blitzkrieg 1940*
BATTLE OF BRITAIN: *The Photographic Kaleidoscope*
BATTLE OF BRITAIN: *The Photopgraphic Kaleidoscope Volume II*
BATTLE OF BRITAIN: *The Photographic Kaleidoscope Volume III*
FIGHTER PILOT: *The Photographic Kaleidoscope*

To receive details of books published by Ramrod Publications, please send to the address shown below.

DOUGLAS BADER: *An Inspiration in Photographs*
© Dilip Sarkar & The Douglas Bader Foundation, 2001

First published 2001 by Ramrod Publications & The Douglas Bader Foundation.
16 Kingfisher Close, St Peter's Park, Worcester WR5 3RY, ENGLAND. Tel & Fax: 01905 767735
Email: anita@ramrodbooks.u-net.com   Website: www.battleofbritain.net/ramrodbooks

ISBN: 0-9538539-1-8

Layout & design by Ramrod Publications
Printed and bound in Great Britain by The Cromwell Press, Trowbridge, Wiltshire.

Acknowledgements

This book could not have been produced without the kind support of a number of people, but in particular Lady Bader, David Bickers and Keith Delderfield of The Douglas Bader Foundation, and Andrew Long who copied certain photographs for reproduction. Larry McHale has, as ever, continued to provide loyal and enthusiastic support.

Our printers, The Cromwell Press, most generously part-sponsored the production costs of this book as a gesture towards the work of The Douglas Bader Foundation.

My wife, Anita, yet again deserves recognition and praise for her essential role in producing my books, and I promise our children, James and Hannah, that one day Daddy will not be quite so busy!

Bibliography

Readers wishing to learn more of Douglas Bader's exploits, and indeed his life and times, may find the following books interesting.

Bader, Sir D: *Fight for the Sky*, Sidgwick & Jackson, 1973.

Brickhill, P: *Reach for the Sky*, William Collins Sons & Co Ltd., 1954.

Dundas, Sir HSL: *Flying Start*, Stanley Paul Ltd, 1988.

Lucas, PB: *Flying Colours: The Epic Story of Douglas Bader*, Stanley Paul Ltd., 1981.

Johnson, JE: *Wing Leader*, Catto & Windus, 1956.

Sarkar, D: *Spitfire Squadron*, Air Research Publications, 1990.

Sarkar, D: *A Few of the Many*, Ramrod Publications, 1995.

Sarkar, D: *Bader's Tangmere Spitfires*, Haynes Publishing (PSL), 1996.

Sarkar, D: *Bader's Duxford Fighters*, Ramrod Publications, 1997.

Sarkar, D: *Battle of Britain: The Photographic Kaleidoscope Vol I-III*, Ramrod Publications, 1999 & 2000.

Sarkar, D: *Fighter Pilot: The Photographic Kaleidoscope*, Ramrod Publications, 2001.

Shores, C & Williams, C: *Aces High*, Grubb Street, 1994.

Contents

Foreword

In the autumn of 1984, whilst serving as an infantry platoon commander in Northern Ireland, I was involved in a booby trap bomb attack and suffered extensive injuries. I lost my left leg above the knee and during almost two months of intensive care, came within hours of having my right leg amputated below the knee. I am thankful for the surgeon's decision to postpone and then cancel the surgery!

I first read 'Reach for the Sky' a few months after leaving intensive care and most vividly remember reading that Douglas had discarded his crutches - I did the same! The book helped me to the perhaps rather obvious conclusion that whatever we put our minds to, even with broken bodies, we can achieve.

My dream was to become a furniture designer and maker. After a course in bench joinery at St Loyes College in Exeter, I completed the very demanding course in wood craftsmanship, design and business at Parnham College in west Dorset. Whilst waiting for a disused cow barn to be converted into my workshop I applied to the Douglas Bader Foundation for help. The very generous grant has enabled me to weather the first two years of being in business and I am now enjoying the pure joy of creating my own designs.

Despite my overriding belief in our ability to achieve I think that we all need a little help some time and the support of the Douglas Bader Foundation was the not so little help that I needed to live my dream...

Andrew V Brown
2001

Nigel Smith

The first memory of Douglas Bader came from my father, for whom Douglas was a wartime hero. I also remember the Colditz story and Reach for the Sky. Douglas was an inspiration not only to those of his own generation, but also to everyone who has ever heard or read of his exploits.

From an early age, my ambition had been to go to sea. Every year my parents would take me on visits to Chatham navy days and, as soon as I was old enough, I joined the Royal Navy. I loved the life, but unfortunately my career was cut short by a road accident in which I lost my right leg above the knee. Discharge was inevitable: it was hard to accept but I always remembered what Douglas Bader had made of his life and he had lost both of his legs.

A few years on I got involved in yachting and in 1996 had the opportunity to sail in the BT Global Challenge Round the World yacht race. The only thing stopping me was the £18,750 berth fee. I applied to the Dougas Bader Foundation for a grant and was accepted. This helped secure my crew place and my dream, a circumnavigation under sail.

Since completing the race, I have not looked back and can be found on the water at every opportunity. I cannot thank the Douglas Bader Foundation enough for their interest and support. They have certainly helped change my life for the better and I am honored that they saw in me someone who, like Douglas Bader, is determined not to let an amputation hamper progress and I am proud that I have been invited to write this foreword.

Long may the charity continue this great mans inspirational work and long may they continue to support many more who, like myself, are seeking success with a new way of life.

Nigel Smith
2001

Author's Introduction

History is punctuated by the names of great men whose positive and often courageous deeds have become legendary. One name amongst the foremost is that of Douglas Bader. Although at one time a world-wide household name, many readers today, unfamiliar with his inspiring story, might legitimately ask 'why?'. The purpose of this book, therefore, is to bring this epic tale back to the fore, in the process promoting the work of the Douglas Bader Foundation, the registered charity founded to uphold the great man as an inspiration to the disabled and provide a facility for amputees.

Although the following section provides a comprehensive overview of Douglas Bader's life and contribution, the photographic presentation is not intended as a fulsome documentary. Supplemented by wartime period photographs from my own archive and certain other sources, the majority of photographs originate from a collection of albums in the possession of Lady Bader, Sir Douglas's widow.

It was a strange feeling, it must be said, sitting in the Berkshire farmhouse once shared by the Baders, sorting through the boxes in which the photographs and other small mementoes of this great man's life had been stored. Out of the boxes came, for example, a letter from the late, also great, actor Kenneth More (who played the star role in the film based upon Douglas Bader's life, *Reach for the Sky*), and an RAF officer's cap badge. To think that the latter was once sewn onto the service cap of none other than Group Captain Bader was amazing! Even more so was to leave with a selection of these photographs and artefacts. Having been effectively entrusted with Sir Douglas Bader's memory was a daunting prospect indeed, not to mention a great honour.

The reader will now be the best judge as to whether the one time schoolboy fascinated and inspired by the Bader legend has done the story justice. What comes through these pages loud and clear, I hope, is that Douglas Bader, a double amputee, led the most fulsome and energetic life imaginable. One thing is for sure: here the tale has not been embellished. Frankly, the story defies even fiction and requires no elaboration on my part.

Dilip Sarkar
Worcester
April 2001

The Bader Factor

An Inspired Lifetime

Douglas Robert Steuart Bader was born on February 21st, 1910, at St John's Wood in London. His father, Frederick, was a Civil Servant and so young Douglas spent his early years in India. The family returned home in 1913, Mr Bader subsequently serving as a major with the Royal Engineers during the Great War. Having remained in France after the armistice, Major Bader eventually succumbed to a wartime head wound and died in 1922. This plunged the family into reduced circumstances, meaning that the 12-year old Douglas, already indicating his potential on the sports field but not an academic, had to work hard to achieve a scholarship to St Edward's School in Oxford. This was perhaps the first major indication of Douglas Bader's determination and resolve.

Before his father's death, Douglas Bader's aunt, Hazel, had married a pilot in the Royal Air Force, Flight Lieutenant Cyril Burge, who had flown throughout most of the Great War with the Royal Flying Corps. Not surprisingly, Master Bader was captivated by his uncle's tales of war in the air. In 1923, Bader stayed with his aunt and uncle at Cranwell, where Burge was the RAF College's first Adjutant. There Bader joined in games with the cadets and sat in the cockpit of an Avro 504 biplane elementary training aircraft. At the end of this visit, the youngster's mind was made up and he determined to eventually return to Cranwell as a Flight Cadet himself. Five years later Douglas Bader did just that and won one of six highly prized King's Cadetships, commencing his course in September 1928.

The RAF College at Cranwell was, in many ways, a cross between a Civil Service staff college, a university, a technical college and a flying school; entrants were actually charged a fee. To ensure that these potential leaders were of only the highest possible standard, and would become educated, cultured and self-assured men destined to become the staff officers and high commanders of the RAF, the Flight Cadet's course was of two years duration and embraced a variety of subjects.

Cranwell captivated Flight Cadet DRS Bader; the ethos of both camaraderie and prestige perfectly suited his personality and background. Bader once more excelled at sport, representing Cranwell at rugby, boxing, cricket and hockey, in addition to playing golf against the College staff.

The exuberance of youth, however, was soon to land Flight Cadet Bader in trouble. He came 19 out of 21 in the end of First Year exams, and that, coupled with a brush with the law over a traffic offence (a misdemeanour also involving Cadets Stephenson, Chance and Field), led to him being carpeted. First he was 'torn off a strip' by his flight commander, Flight Lieutenant MacFadyen, then, much worse, by the College Commandant, Air Vice-Marshal Halahan. The latter told him in no uncertain terms that the Air Force required men, *not* boys. From that moment on, Bader was forced to transform his attitude and outlook at Cranwell in order to justify his place there.

In his Second Year, Bader commenced flying Siskins, his ambition being to become a fighter pilot.

Although still relentlessly pursuing his sporting interests, perhaps surprisingly Bader's groundwork also improved. At that time, Squadron Leader Rupert Leigh was a First Year student: -

To us Bader was a sort of god who played every conceivable game and was the best player in every team.

Having passed out of Cranwell (Bader having been beaten narrowly into second place for the Sword of Honour), on August 25th, 1930, Pilot Officers DRS Bader and GD Stephenson reported for duty to fly Gloster Gamecock biplane fighters with 23 Squadron at Kenley. The following day, Bader made his first flight proper as a fighter pilot, in Gamecock J8084: 'Landings, take-offs, local flying. First solo.' He flew twice more that day, both sorties described in his logbook as 'landings, take-offs and aerobatics'; it was at aerobatics that Bader was to excel. Throughout this time, his flying was predominantly formation and aerobatics practice, often in company with his Cranwell friend Stephenson. On August 23rd, 1930, Bader wrote in his logbook: 'Landed (on nose!) at Sidcup owing to mist and rain.'

The aerobatic abilities of Pilot Officers Bader and Stephenson, the former a daredevil exponent of the slow roll at low altitude, was recognised at Kenley, and from April in 1931 onwards, Bader's log book records numerous flights practising for the Hendon Air Pageant. In June, Flight Lieutenant Harry Day, the 'C' Flight Commander, selected Pilot Officer Bader as his No 2 in Hendon's pairs aerobatics competition. 23 Squadron's pair, with Pilot Officer Stephenson as the reserve pilot, won the competition, described by the *Times* as 'the event of the day.' On August 20th, 1931 - one year after Pilot Officer Bader had reported for duty with 23 Squadron - Flight Lieutenant Day led the aerobatics team on a flight from Kenley to Cramlington, near Newcastle, stopping to refuel at Cranwell and Catterick. En route to Cramlington, however, Bader had dropped out of formation and hedgehopped for an hour, well below the regulation height for low flying. This act incurred the wrath of Flight Lieutenant Day. Bader had been warned.

In 1931, Bader also pursued his sporting ambitions with great zeal, playing both cricket and rugby for the RAF, and the latter also for the Harlequins, Surrey, and the Combined Services Team. Bader's place as fly half in the full England international squad looked assured.

Low aerobatics continued to be a problem for 23 Squadron. One pilot was killed in such circumstances, followed soon after by another. Harry Day, temporarily commanding the squadron (during which time Flying Officer Stephenson signed Bader's log book as 'Officer Commanding "C" Flight'), called his pilots together and lectured them on low aerobatics in the Bristol Bulldog, 23 Squadron's new mount. Referring to the height of 2,000 feet for aerobatics stipulated by Fighting Area regulations, Day indicated that he was prepared to allow *some* latitude; Day's job was to turn out pilots who had courage and judgement for war, and his advice was sound. Pilot Officer Bader ignored this further warning, however, and in November was reported for 'beating up' the aerodrome. Day rightly considered that the 20-year old Bader, in the wake of his Hendon and sporting successes, was becoming over-confident. Air Commodore Mermagen commented that 'he was a real show off, he could do everything brilliantly, but did it very low'.

On December 14th, 1931, Pilot Officer Bader's Bristol Bulldog biplane joined two other 23 Squadron aircraft on a social flight to Woodley airfield, near Reading. Not surprisingly Bader, the Hendon star, was the subject of much attention in the clubhouse. Pilot Officer Bader took off and commenced

a series of very low rolls over the airfield. Suddenly his left wing brushed the ground and within seconds the Bulldog became a bent and twisted mass of wreckage. Within the cockpit, Douglas Bader lay terribly injured. His right leg was consequently amputated above the knee and the left below. In his pilot's flying logbook, he later wrote: -

X Country Reading. Crashed slow rolling near ground. Bad show.

A 'bad show' it certainly was, although, as Lady Bader recounted in 1996, 'he knew that it was his own bloody silly fault and that was that'. Indeed, many years later Douglas himself passed comment on the accident that changed the course of his life, 'Just made a balls of it, old boy. That's all there was to it!'.

As Douglas himself later said, 'The fact remains that I lost my two legs at the age of 21 and went through the same pain and grief in the first few weeks and months that everyone else has experienced in similar conditions'.

In those first few weeks, Douglas came to terms with the fact that he no longer had legs. The priority then was not to walk again, but to get physically strong once more. Eventually, he did so and was able to try out artificial legs for the first time; the following quote is extracted from some previously unpublished notes written by Douglas himself: -

The biggest disappointment that I had was the initial difficulty of trying to operate the artificial legs when I first got them. Having always been of an athletic nature and knowing nothing about artificial legs I thought during my convalescence that once I got them I should wander around after a day or two quite normally. When I went for my first fitting of these legs and actually put them on and tried to stand up in them, I never thought that I would move them. With a strong man each side of me, having been levered to my feet, I stood there as far as I was concerned nailed to the ground with no conscious balance if I let go of my two supporters. After a certain amount of time, trouble and a great deal of sweat I began to get some inkling of how to operate the artificial knee of the right leg.

After battling away for several days during the course of which I spent a good deal of time on the ground, my mind and my reflexes gradually acquired the method of movement needed, and then as always it suddenly came with a rush and did not seem so difficult.

Douglas had to achieve not only independence of mobility, but also in respect of every day tasks that the able-bodied take for granted. He continues: -

My morning routine is to get up, get on to the floor and go along by the hands and backside method to the bathroom where there is a chair or stool beside the bath. With one hand on the edge of the bath and one on the stool you seat yourself on the latter. With one hand on the stool and one on the edge of the bath you raise yourself and sit on the edge of the bath and then with a hand on each side of the bath you lower yourself into the bathtub. Having slipped off the edge once and hurt yourself, you remember to put a wet face flannel on the nearest side of the bathtub on which you are going to sit before getting into the bath. This stops you slipping. You only need to forget it once and you will remember it for the rest of your life. The same thing applies to getting out. You seat yourself on the face flannel on the edge of the bath and then on the stool. If you have left your legs in the bathroom the night before, they are there for you to put on and walk away from the bathroom in the morning. If you are married you can leave your legs in the bedroom at night and your wife can bring them along to the bathroom in the morning.

It is in overcoming the ordinary day-to-day requirements like the above that a disabled person achieves normality. If you cannot wash yourself and have a bath and do all the essential everyday requirements of life without someone to help you, you are inevitably restricted and the aim of every disabled person is to be completely independent. If you have

achieved that, you have achieved normality. You can travel all over the world, visit out of the way places and lead a similar life to anyone else without ever being a nuisance to other people or yourself. To my way of thinking, a disabled person who achieves independence is no longer disabled.

Douglas Bader 'achieved independence' and, remarkably, on September 29th, 1937, just nine months after the crash that left him legless, he flew again. The flight lasting 25 minutes was as a passenger in an Avro 504, flown by a Flight Lieutenant Leach, at the Central Flying School (CFS). Soon afterwards he piloted a machine himself: -

Flying an aeroplane presents no difficulty unless it is equipped with foot brakes. Before the war all British aeroplanes were equipped with a rudder control which was either a bar pivoted in the middle (so that pressure by either foot swung the bar) or there were two complete foot pedals which moved up and down. You pushed with your right foot for right rudder and vice versa. Now, if you place your foot on a bar and push you can do that from your thigh and your shin without having to depress your foot in relation to your skin. The brakes on aeroplanes in those days were operated from the control column or joystick by means of a lever rather like that on the handle bar of a motorcycle. When you depressed the lever and the rudder bar was central, both brakes went on. You obtained differential braking by moving the rudder bar on whichever side you wanted the brake, i.e. right rudder, right brake.

Not surprisingly, however, King's Regulations contained no reference to pilots without legs, so the service ultimately refused to allow Bader to continue flying. On April 30th, 1933, Flying Officer DRS Bader was retired 'on the grounds of ill health'. Benumbed, having been forced to quit the service he loved so much, Bader started work in the office of the Asiatic Petroleum Company's aviation department, hardly a fair exchange for the cockpit of a Bulldog. Denied of aerobatics, he found his thrills behind the wheel of a fast sports car which he apparently often drove with little regard for other road users: two accidents resulted.

With an annual salary of £200, on October 5th, 1933, Douglas married Thelma Edwards (a cousin of the Donaldson brothers who were all to later achieve fame in the wartime RAF). Desperately missing both flying and service life, however, the 23-year old amputee also missed sport. Golf was a game that the determined Douglas thought that he could play on equal terms with able-bodied men, so it was off to the golf course for the newly weds. The first swing at a ball was not a success: Douglas ignominiously fell on his backside. Nevertheless persistence was rewarded and before too long he was competing and, importantly for Douglas, winning. Later, he wrote of the importance of golf: -

Golf undoubtedly is the game that a physically handicapped person can play on equal terms with others. The great thing about golf is that you can play it anywhere. Whether you have one arm or no legs or whatever it is, the handicapping system is such that you can always have a good game and a lot of fun. I would say that it is probably the game that is played most by disabled people in preference to any other. I have met some splendid one-armed players and ones with legs missing. When I first started this game I used to swing the club very fast and fell over every time, but after a bit I discovered that swinging slowly and gripping the club lightly enabled me to keep my arms clear of my body and therefore avoid upsetting my balance. I still over-balance occasionally but so does everybody else. Only on rare occasions does one get a stance, for instance in the left-hand corner of a bunker, which is more difficult for a disabled man than the ordinary chap, the reason being that you cannot take weight on your above-knee leg when it is bent.

By the time that his golf handicap had been reduced to a very respectable nine, the clouds of war were gathering once more over Europe. Recognising war as his salvation, however, Douglas Bader welcomed every aggressive move made by Germany. Immediately after the Munich Crisis in 1938,

realising that trained service pilots would be in demand and seeing this as his chance, Douglas wrote to the Air Ministry offering his services and requested a refresher-flying course. The answer was negative but tempered with the offer of a commission in the administrative branch, which he flatly refused.

In April 1939, when Hitler's troops marched into the guaranteed portion of Czechoslovakia, Douglas tried again. On August 31st, 1939, Air Vice-Marshal Charles Portal, the Air Member for Personnel, replied to yet another request confirming that, provided the doctors agreed, in the event of war he would be used in a flying capacity. On September 1st, 1939, Nazi Germany invaded Poland. Two days later, Hitler having ignored their ultimatum to remove his forces forthwith, Britain and France declared war on Germany. Due to the geography involved, however, Britain and France were unable to send military aid to Poland, which soon surrendered after a vain but gallant fight. Nevertheless, Douglas Bader saw his chance and seized the day with both hands.

Air Vice-Marshal Halahan, Cranwell's Commandant in Flight Cadet Bader's day, then paved the way for his former student to rejoin the service. Halahan sent the medical board a note explaining that he had known Bader at Cranwell and could confirm that he was just the sort of spirited officer now required. Declared fit for flying duties, Bader's next stop was the CFS.

When Douglas Bader arrived there on October 18th, 1939, he was delighted to find that the commander of the Refresher Squadron's 'A' Flight, who was to undertake his flying assessment, was none other than Rupert Leigh, now a Squadron Leader but previously his junior at Cranwell. Leigh, by his own admission, considered Bader a 'God'. What Douglas Bader felt as he clambered back into the cockpit of one of His Majesty's aircraft can only be imagined. A few minutes later he landed, finding it hard to believe that he had ever been away. His elation at successfully completing the test can only be imagined.

On November 27th, 1939, Flying Officer Douglas Bader returned again to the CFS and reported for duty to the Refresher Squadron. In his new logbook, Bader carried over 'Approximately 500 hours solo'. Later that day he made his first flight, following his return to the service, as a passenger in an Avro Tutor flown by an instructor, Flight Lieutenant Clarkson. The next flight was a solo on the same type, during which he flew an *inverted* circuit of the aerodrome. On December 2nd, Squadron Leader Leigh was again the '1st Pilot' in Harvard N7184, Flying Officer Bader being his passenger. Although the latter could never solo on this type, because of the foot brakes, it remained imperative that he accumulated experience on the Harvard due to its comparatively high performance and prior to flying one of the new, fast monoplane fighters that were completely new to him. On December 4th, Bader flew Fairey Battle N2254, a monoplane light bomber powered by a Rolls-Royce Merlin engine, and on the 10th, Squadron Leader Leigh again flew with him in the Harvard. On December 20th, 1939, Flying Officer DRS Bader soloed in Hawker Hurricane L1873, undertaking 'Circuits and landings and *low-flying*'. I doubt whether he could have had a better Christmas present.

At the time, Group Captain Alfred B Woodhall was 'Squadron Leader Flying Ops.' at the Duxford Sector Station in 12 Group. 'Woody' remembered: -

One day, Douglas Bader flew over from the CFS in a Hurricane. I was delighted and amazed to see him, as I had not

done so since his crash. He was in terrific form, and as it happened the AOC also came to visit us. I introduced Douglas to the AOC, and over lunch Douglas used all his considerable charm in persuading Leigh-Mallory to take him into one of his operational squadrons. After lunch, with the AOC watching, Douglas put on a most finished display of aerobatics, and this finally decided 'L-M'. Douglas was posted almost at once to No 19 Squadron, at Duxford, commanded by his old friend and term-mate from Cranwell, Geoffrey Stephenson. Douglas impressed us all with his terrific personality and his amazing keenness and drive. I have never known his equal. Flying was his supreme passion and his enthusiasm infected us all.

As a spectator, I was intrigued to see the impact that Douglas Bader had on the AOC - and vice-versa. Air Vice-Marshal and Flying Officer, rank did not enter into it. They were two of a kind - born leaders. They were both men who were respected by all, and were affectionately esteemed by most. Their attraction for each other was immediate, and their friendship was, I am sure, established at that first meeting.

On February 7th, 1940, Flying Officer DRS Bader left the CFS upon posting to fly Spitfires with 19 (F) Squadron at Duxford: he was home again at last. Flying Officer Douglas Bader became a member of 'A' Flight, commanded by Flight Lieutenant Brian Lane. Bader first flew a Spitfire, K9853, on February 12th, 1940.

Air Vice-Marshal Michael Lyne, then a young Pilot Officer, remembered: -

By March the weather was better, but we now had Flying Officer Douglas Bader to contend with. He was very brave and determined but was having a hard time coming to grips with the Spitfire, a far more advanced machine than the biplanes he had flown when previously an RAF fighter pilot. He particularly experienced problems in cloud. More than once my friend Watson and I, both Pilot Officers, were lent to Bader as a formation by the CO but emerged from cloud faithfully following our leader only to find ourselves in a steep diving turn!

Throughout March 1940, 19 Squadron deployed a section of three aircraft to Horsham St Faith, in Norfolk, on a daily basis to provide convoy protection patrols. Michael Lyne recalls the events of March 31st: -

On this occasion, Douglas Bader was leading our section, which also included Pilot Officer Watson, and we went off downwind on the shortest run at Horsham. Douglas, however, forgot to put the airscrew into fine pitch for take-off, and cartwheeled across the main road and into a ploughed field. Watson and I stuck with him until the last minute but then pulled up and away on emergency power. I remember only just clearing the hedge and seeing clods of earth flying high overhead from my leader's Spitfire. Bader broke a pair of artificial legs in the accident, in fact, and had to send away for a new pair.

Flying Officer Bader's Spitfire, K9858, was written off. Surprisingly, on the same day, Squadron Leader Stephenson wrote in Bader's logbook 'Ability as a Spitfire pilot Exceptional.' Nevertheless, Bader was unhappy in 19 Squadron, particularly with his status as a Flying Officer. Duxford's other Spitfire squadron, 222, was commanded by Squadron Leader HW 'Tubby' Mermagen, who, as Bader himself later wrote, 'was an exact contemporary of mine. We used to play rugby together'; Air Commodore Mermagen remembered: -

When I was commanding 222 Squadron at RAF Duxford during 1939/40, Douglas Bader, a personal friend, was serving alongside us in 19 Squadron. However, he was finding it difficult to serve under Squadron Leader Geoffrey Stephenson, with whom he had once shared equal rank at Kenley before his accident. Bader knew that I had a flight commander who was suspected of being lacking in moral fibre whom I wished to get rid of. Bader therefore asked me if I would approach the AOC, Leigh-Mallory, regarding the possibility of him being transferred to 222 as a flight commander. The AOC agreed.

On April 16th, 1940, Douglas Bader was promoted to Acting Flight Lieutenant and assumed command of 222 Squadron's 'A' Flight. The so-called 'Phoney War' was soon to be at end, however: in the spring of 1940, Hitler successfully invaded Norway and Denmark. Then came the long awaited *blitzkrieg* against the west. On May 10th, German forces invaded neutral Holland, Belgium and Luxembourg, and France. German armour penetrated the supposedly impassable Ardennes forest, out flanking the much-vaunted French Maginot Line in the process. Although the Allied armies, including the British Expeditionary Force, which won five Victoria Crosses, fought doggedly and valiantly, ultimately the campaign ended in defeat. Those Allied forces that could be saved were evacuated from the beaches of Dunkirk, leaving behind their transport, armour and artillery.

On May 28th, 1940, 222 Squadron flew south to Hornchurch in Essex, from where it contributed with air operations covering the Dunkirk evacuation. In the dangerous skies over the French coast, Spitfires and Me 109s clashed for the first time. Amongst those young British pilots trying their very best to offer some protection to the hard-pressed troops below was Flight Lieutenant Douglas Bader.

On June 1st, Flight Lieutenant Bader scored his first victory when he destroyed an Me109 and damaged an Me 110 over Dunkirk. Air Commodore Mermagen recalled that sortie: -

When we landed, Douglas stomped over to me and enthused, 'I got five for certain, Tubby, old boy!' Now this was the first time we had met Me 109s, which were damn good aeroplanes, and everything happened very quickly indeed. To be certain of having destroyed five enemy aircraft in such circumstances was impossible. I said 'You're a bloody liar, Bader!' We credited him with one destroyed. Nevertheless, Bader was generally easy to keep in order, as it were, and he had already proved to be an excellent flight commander. He carried out several operational sorties under my command and displayed exceptional leadership qualities; he was a fine Spitfire pilot. He used to come stomping into dispersal saying 'Come on chaps, get out of the way, I want a cup of coffee', barging everyone else aside, but the chaps loved him for it, he was a real morale booster.

The Squadron flew over Dunkirk again on June 1st. The bloodthirsty Flying Officer Bader returned safely to write in his logbook: 'Attacked two Heinkel 111s. Killed one rear gunner and damaged machine.'

By June 3rd, the Dunkirk evacuation was considered complete, and air operations over the French coast came to an end.

Back at Duxford, on June 12th, Flight Lieutenant Bader flew an 'R/T test for AOC' when Air Vice-Marshal Leigh-Mallory visited the Sector Operations Room. The following day, Bader crashed on landing after a night patrol in Spitfire 'ZD-D'; Air Commodore Mermagen: -

On that occasion Douglas came in far too high and far too fast. He went through a hedge. I drove over to pick him up and he was ranting, shouting that the flarepath was incorrectly laid out. I thought, 'Well look at that, what a total lack of humility, he's blaming someone else now!'

That Spitfire was badly damaged.

Despite this further accident, on June 23rd, Squadron Leader Mermagen wrote in Bader's logbook: 'Assessment as a fighter pilot on Spitfires Exceptional'. The following day, Douglas Bader was

promoted to Acting Squadron Leader. Having returned as a fighter pilot for just four months, he had risen from lowly Flying Officer to Squadron Leader.

This promotion was, of course, despite several blameworthy crashes; even Bader, concerned regarding this spate of flying accidents, was surprised himself.

As we have seen, by this time 'Woody' Woodhall was the Station Commander at Duxford: -

Soon after the fall of France, Leigh-Mallory rang me to say that No 242 Squadron (Canadian) were reporting to Coltishall and would be under the operational control of the Duxford Sector. He told me that the squadron had had a tough time in France, and that the groundcrews had just been evacuated via Cherbourg, thanks to the resources of their adjutant, Flight Lieutenant Peter MacDonald MP. Their own CO had left them to their own devices after the pilots had landed in England, and the squadron, led by Flying Officer Stan Turner, had landed at Coltishall with nothing but the uniforms they were wearing. Tools, spares, kit, baggage - the lot had had to be abandoned.

LM said 'I've got to find them a new squadron commander but he's got to be good because these chaps are Canadians and they've had a rough time - they are browned off with authority and need a good leader - any suggestions?'

At once, I said 'What about Douglas Bader?'

LM replied 'I thought you'd say that. I think you are right.'

On June 24th, 1940, Acting Squadron Leader Bader therefore arrived at Coltishall where he immediately led by both example and deed. Upon arrival at Coltishall, he took off in Hurricane P2967, later describing the sortie of 1 hour 10 minutes as 'Practice on type'. In fact, 242's new CO executed a breathtaking display of aerobatics, proving the point that he was as good a flyer as any able-bodied pilot. He then rapidly gathered his men about him, having his friend, Flight Lieutenant Eric Ball, posted from 19 Squadron to command 'A' Flight in 242, and Flight Lieutenant George Powell-Sheddon, also an Old Cranwellian, to command 'B' Flight.

Group Captain Woodhall: -

242 Squadron soon became an enthusiastic team led by their single-minded and swashbuckling CO, Douglas Bader.

Squadron Leader Bader initially commenced an intensive regime of training flying, but on July 4th, 1940, he signalled 12 Group, with a copy to Fighter Command, to the effect that 242 Squadron was operational in terms of pilots trained for day flying, but 'non-operational as regards equipment'. It was definitely not 'done' for a newly promoted *Acting* Squadron Leader to send such a signal to Fighter Command HQ, but by having done so Bader had cleverly engineered a situation that required resolution. Squadron Leader Bader consequently argued with an HQ equipment officer of equal rank, after which Air Chief Marshal Dowding, The AOC-in-Chief of Fighter Command, requested Bader's presence at Bentley Priory. After the somewhat forthright CO of 242 Squadron stated his case, Dowding moved swiftly, sacking the equipment officer and ordering forthwith Squadron Leader Bader's requirements. Needless to say, the incident earned Bader great respect amongst 242 Squadron personnel.

On July 9th, 1940, just one day before the Battle of Britain officially commenced, 242 Squadron became *fully* operational.

No one, least of all Hitler's generals, had expected France to fall so soon. This changed everything. Flying from bases in the Pas-de-Calais, this meant that German fighters could now escort and protect *Luftwaffe* bombers attacking targets in England. Even London itself was in their (albeit limited) range. With the summer ahead, Hitler now had the opportunity to crush RAF Fighter Command as a prelude to a seaborne invasion. Having enjoyed unprecedented success on the continent, the Germans were sublimely confident. *Reichsmarschal* Hermann Göring, Commander-in-Chief of the German Air Force, boasted that the RAF would be defeated in 'three weeks'. Fighter Command's Commander-in-Chief, despite being numerically outnumbered, thought otherwise, believing that he could hold out 'indefinitely'. As the British Prime Minister, Winston Churchill, told the British people, 'The Battle of France is over. I expect that the Battle of Britain is about to begin'. The eyes of the world were now focussed upon the forthcoming air battle, which would not only decide the fate of beleaguered Britain but also the free world.

Officially, the Battle of Britain is considered to have started on July 10th, 1940. By this time, the fighter squadron's of Fighter Command's No 11 Group, protecting London and the south east, were already engaged in bitter combat with enemy fighters and bombers over Channel bound convoys. These early skirmishes often involved over 100 whirling, duelling fighters, but by comparison 12 Group's war was already mundane. Protecting the industrial Midlands and the north, the most Air Vice-Marshal Leigh-Mallory's eager pilots could hope for was a brush with either an east coastal convoy raider or lone reconnaissance aircraft.

Throughout the morning of July 11th, 1940, German reconnaissance aircraft constantly monitored British coastal waters: over 80 such sorties were plotted by radar stations from the north of Scotland to Land's End. One of these flights was undertaken at dawn by a Do 17 of *Wettererkundungsstaffel 261*, briefed to report on weather conditions off the Norfolk and Suffolk coasts. Off Yarmouth at 0600 hrs Squadron Leader Rupert Leigh and Sergeant Reg Hyde of 66 Squadron intercepted the intruder. Having damaged the oil tank of Leigh's Spitfire, however, the Do 17 escaped into cloud.

The Group Controller also ordered Squadron Leader Bader to scramble a section of 242 Squadron Hurricanes against this particular 'Bogey'. Bader declined, due to the bad weather conditions, but agreed to go alone. Consequently and shortly after 66 Squadron's inconclusive contact, the Dornier concerned was intercepted off Cromer by Squadron Leader Bader. Between clouds, he managed a long burst at the enemy aircraft, which silenced the rear gunner, but was frustrated to lose the bomber in another cloud. At 0610 hrs, the Dornier crashed into the sea, 242 Squadron thus chalking up its first kill: the new CO had proved himself in combat.

Throughout the latter half of August 1940, the tempo of battle increased. Extensive aerial reconnaissance of southern England was followed by heavy attacks on shipping, ports and installations, radar stations, and, towards the end, by strikes along the south coast and, in particular, Fighter Command's airfields. 11 Group continued to bear the brunt of the fighting, those Squadrons in 12 Group still largely occupied with chasing lone raiders or, much more mundanely, providing endless protection patrols for convoys travelling around the coasts of eastern England.

At Coltishall, Squadron Leader Douglas Bader was not content to while away his time playing games of patience. He sulked and stormed, unable to accept that his was a lesser part in what was clearly a

critical aerial conflict. Together with his pilots of 242 Squadron, he sat restlessly at readiness, eagerly awaiting the scramble call that never seemed to come. For a man with such an irrepressible spirit and constant thirst for action as Douglas Bader, being kept out of the battle was intolerable. Directly, and contrarily to the provisions of the System of Air Defence, Bader frequently pressured his friends, Wing Commander Woodhall, the Sector Controller, and even the AOC, Air Vice-Marshal Leigh-Mallory, directly, imploring that his Squadron be sent into action over 11 Group's area. Under the provisions of the System, however, such a move was impossible until 11 Group called for assistance.

Air Marshal Sir Denis Crowley-Milling remembered: -

Naturally Douglas wanted to get us of 242 Squadron into the action. He used to say 'Why don't they get us airborne when the Germans were building up over the Pas-de-Calais?' He felt that we could then proceed south and meet the enemy formation on its way in.

What 12 Group's pilots generally failed to appreciate was that they were there as a part of Dowding's *overall* defence, with the Group having its own area of geographical responsibility in addition to the task of reinforcing 11 Group if so required. Although the Commander-in-Chief had delegated the tactical initiative to his Group Commanders, he retained the broad perspective concerning Fighter Command as a whole. A heavy attack could have developed at any time on the Midlands or north of England, in which case 12 Group's pilots would have quenched their thirst for action.

On August 15th, the Germans not only made heavy attacks on targets in southern England, but also attacked the north in strength. Unfortunately for Squadron Leader Bader, 242 Squadron was not involved, and the following day it was the 12 Group 19 Squadron that enjoyed combat success. That day, Squadron Leader Bader himself had been vectored to intercept two 'X-Raids', but both, as so often happened in what was, after all, Bomber Command country, transpired to be friendly aircraft. We can only wonder at his mounting frustration: not only was the battle raging in southern England, but what action was to be enjoyed over 12 Group was largely being had by other squadrons.

A new phase in the aerial conflict began on August 19th, 1940, and lasted until September 5th. During this time, the emphasis of enemy attacks concentrated on inland aerodromes and aircraft factories, industrial targets and, according to Air Vice-Marshal Park, the AOC 11 Group, 'areas which could only be classified as residential'

The tactic used by Air Vice-Marshal Park against the enemy bombers was essentially one of forward interception whereby his fighters met the enemy as far forward as possible, whilst the bombers were en route to their target. In the event of all of Park's forces being engaged, and in accordance with the System, 12 Group was to supply squadrons to patrol over and protect the 11 Group airfields north of the Thames.

On August 21st, whilst leading 242 Squadron home from a practice flight, on the R/T Squadron Leader Bader heard Squadron Leader Rupert Leigh's 66 Squadron being vectored onto a 'Bogey' over Yarmouth at 7,000 feet. Bader immediately detached himself from his squadron and sped the 15 miles to Yarmouth. In his logbook, he wrote: -

Intercepted Do 17 above cloud whilst flying alone. Hit it but saw no result as he dived into cloud.

Although Squadron Leader Bader made no claim after the inconclusive combat, he later added: -

Subsequently confirmed crashed in sea. Crew killed.

By this time, of course, bitter fighting had been ongoing over southern England for over a month, throughout which time 12 Group's pilots had been asking '*why* don't they call *us*?' They knew just how hard-pressed their comrades in 11 Group appeared to be.

By August 30th, 1940, the *Luftwaffe's* attacks against Great Britain had grown more ferocious still. No 11 Group's airfields increasingly became the German bombers' targets; the Battle of Britain was entering its most critical phase.

At around 1100 hrs that morning, after the enemy had made a forward fighter sweep in strength, the Observer Corps reported waves, consisting of over 100 'bandits' coming in over the south-east coast, these splitting up over Kent and Surrey to attack the airfields at Biggin Hill and Eastchurch. As the high explosives cascaded down, another wave of enemy bombers crossed the Sussex coast, fighting its way north.

The scale of fighting was such that Air Vice-Marshal Leigh-Mallory decided that one of Coltishall's squadrons was also required to be at Readiness in the Duxford Sector: 242 Squadron. This was it, at last! To Squadron Leader Bader's great chagrin, however, whilst en route to Duxford, 242 Squadron was recalled to Coltishall. Fuming, 242's CO 'harangued Ops over the phone'. Later, 242 was ordered off again and arrived at Duxford without further incident.

At about 1600 hrs, 300 plus enemy aircraft were reported over Kent and the Thames Estuary. The raiders split up to attack the airfields at Kenley, North Weald, Hornchurch, Debden, Lympne, Detling and Biggin Hill. At 1620 hrs, 60 He 111s of I/KG1 and II/KG53, escorted by Me 110s, crossed the coast north of the Thames. No doubt expecting the enemy to attack those airfields in that vicinity, the 11 Group Controller, via HQ Fighter Command, immediately requested assistance from 12 Group.

At 1623 hrs, Wing Commander Woodhall, the 12 Group Controller and Duxford Station Commander, scrambled 242 Squadron. Consequently Squadron Leader Bader led 14 Hurricanes off from Duxford with orders to patrol North Weald at 15,000 feet.

At about the time of 242 Squadron's scramble, the incoming enemy formation split in two, I/KG1 heading for the Vauxhall Motor Works and aerodrome at Luton, whilst II/KG53, now the larger of the two formations, commenced fighting its way to the Handley Page factory at Radlett.

The official 242 Squadron combat report relates that: -

Squadron 242 were ordered at 1623 hrs from Duxford to patrol North Weald at 15,000' on a vector 190 degrees just north of North Weald. They received a vector of 340 degrees. Three aircraft were noticed to the right of the formation, so the Squadron Leader detached Blue Section to investigate.

These three aircraft were almost certainly friendly Blenheims also reported by No 1 Squadron. The

Coltishall Sector Intelligence Officer, Flight Lieutenant Maybaum, continues:-

Green Leader then drew attention to a large enemy formation on their left so the rest of the squadron turned and saw a vast number of aeroplanes flying in an easterly direction. These were recognised to be from 70-100 E/A, twin-engined in tight formation, stepped up at 12,000', after which there was a gap of 1,000', then another swarm of twin-engined machines stepped up from about 15,000 - 20,000'.

Squadron Leader Bader's own report, also dated September 2nd confirms that: -

242 Squadron was flying in sections line astern at 15,000' when large enemy formation was sighted on the left. 242 Squadron had the height advantage on the lower group and as it was obviously impossible to attack all the enemy it was decided to attack down sun on the lower group.

The sight of so many enemy aircraft must have been incredible for Squadron Leader Bader and his pilots, this being reflected by the 242 Squadron combat report that describes the quantity as 'vast'. However, the 11 Group squadrons now also known to have been involved made no comment to indicate that this raid was anything other than the size they were used to encountering.

Maybaum's report continued: -

Green Section were ordered to attack the top of the lower formation; Red and Yellow Sections were ordered to get into line astern. It seemed impossible to order any formation attack. The Squadron Leader dived straight into the middle of the formation closely followed by Red Two and Red Three; the packed formation broke up and a dogfight ensued. Squadron Leader Bader saw three Me 110s do climbing turns to the left and three to the right. Their tactics appeared to be to climb in turns until they were nearly stalling above the tail of Squadron Leader Bader's aircraft. Squadron Leader Bader fired a short burst into the Me 110 at practically point blank range and the E/A burst into flames and disintegrated almost immediately. Squadron Leader Bader continued his zoom and saw another Me 110 below and so turned in behind it and got a very easy shot at about 100 to 150 yards range. After the E/A had received Squadron Leader Bader's first burst of from 2 to 4 seconds, the enemy pilot avoided further action by putting the stick violently backwards and forwards.

Squadron Leader Bader got another burst in and saw pieces of the enemy's starboard wing fly off; then the whole starboard wing went on fire and E/A went down burning in a spiral dive. Squadron Leader Bader then saw in his mirror another Me 110; he did a quick turn and noticed 5 or 6 white streams coming out of forward-firing guns; the E/A immediately put his nose down and was lost but subsequently seen far below.

Squadron Leader Bader saw nothing around him, called Duxford and was told to land.

Red Two Pilot Officer WC McKnight went into attack with Squadron Leader Bader; he got behind an Me 110 and opened fire at 100 yards, the E/A burst into flames and crashed to the ground. Next he attacked an He 111 formation, carrying out a beam attack on nearest one; E/A rolled over on back, port engine caught fire and it finally crashed to the ground. P/O McKnight was then being attacked by an Me 110 but succeeded in getting behind and followed E/A from 10,000' to 1,000'. P/O McKnight opened fire at about 30 yards; E/A's starboard engine stopped; the port engine caught fire and E/A crashed in flames alongside a large reservoir.

Red 3 P/O Crowley-Milling also went into attack with Red 1 and 2. Seeing an He 111 break away from the formation he made an astern attack giving a five second burst. The enemy did not avoid action, but rear gunfire was experienced. Starboard engine of E/A started to smoke then E/A made dive to the ground. At this particular moment an Me 110 was commencing an attack so did not observe He 111 crash, though P/O Hart confirms seeing this aircraft going down in flames.

Yellow 1 F/Lt GE Ball sighted an He 111 diving and turning and gave him a third of his ammunition.

P/O Stansfield was also attacking this a/c which went down with engines alight and went down on an aerodrome full of cars. F/Lt Ball then attacked an Me 110, making a port attack finishing with a stern attack. One engine stopped dead and no return fire was experienced .... the sun was behind in both attacks.

Yellow 2 Sub/Lt Cork, Royal Navy, saw an Me 110 which he attacked in company with several others and which he saw going down, he broke away and saw another Me 110 flying east, made a beam attack noticing port engine in flames. E/A did a stalled turn and dived to ground.

Yellow 3, Sgt Lonsdale attacked an He 111 which had broken away from its formation. After a prolonged burst of fire from quarter attack, E/A circled and crashed in flames, made no evasive tactics.

Green 1, F/O Christie was with his section attacking a higher formation of E/A when he sighted an He 111 and 3 Me 110s. He carried out a head on attack on 1 Me 110. E/A dived to port. He then attacked from astern, damaging starboard motor, then gave him two-quarter attacks. Finally causing E/A to dive from 2,000' crashing into a greenhouse 500 yards west of Welsh Harp Lake. One short burst from rear gunner, but no effect.

Green 3, P/O Hart saw 3 He 111s below him and started to dive on them. He saw Yellow 1 attacking the last one and so attacked the second, which went into a steep dive. He was about to follow the first E/A, which started a right hand turn. He turned inside the E/A and gave him all his ammunition. E/A plunged downwards in flames and crashed in a field.

White 2, Sgt Brimble, was flying at the rear of the sqn and after E/A formation had been broken saw an He 111 which he gave a burst of 3 secs. P/O Stansfield was also attacking this a/c and followed it to the ground. White 2 then broke away and saw behind him an Me 110 doing a gentle turn to port. He made a quarter attack opening fire for 3 seconds at 250 yards. E/A immediately burst into flames and crashed to the ground. On rejoining his leader he saw another Me 110 commencing an attack on his a/c from the front. He opened fire, finally making a quarter attack, noticing the glass in front of E/A splinter and machine go into a violent dive. He did not see the a/c crash as another 110 was on his tail but feels certain that the pilot was dead.

Although there were, in fact, many other RAF fighters involved, 242 Squadron's perception was that it alone had inflicted great losses on the enemy. The Squadron claimed seven Me 110s destroyed and three probables, and five He 111s destroyed. At the time, these claims were accepted, and Air Vice-Marshal Leigh-Mallory sent a signal to the squadron: 'Heartiest congratulations on a first-class show. Well done 242.' The Chief of the Air Staff added his congratulations: 'Magnificent fighting. You are well on top of the enemy and obviously the fine Canadian traditions of the last war are safe in your hands.' The Under-Secretary of State for Air also sent 242 a similar message.

The engagement naturally sent morale soaring in 242 Squadron, and their limbless Squadron Leader assumed God like proportions.

The perceived success of 242 Squadron on August 30th, 1940, led Douglas Bader to consider tactics:

When we were writing out our combat reports afterwards, Leigh-Mallory rang me up and said "congratulations, Bader, on the Squadron's performance today". I said "Thank you very much, Sir, but if we'd had more aeroplanes then we could have shot down a whole lot more". He asked what I meant and I explained that with more fighters our results would have been even better. He agreed, in principal and created the 'Duxford Wing', under my leadership, (firstly) comprising three squadrons, 242, 310 and 19. Leigh-Mallory said to try the idea and see what we could do.

The 'Wing' saw action for the first time on September 7th, 1940, and again made many combat claims. Building upon this success, other 12 Group units, 611, 616 and 302, joined the 'Big Wing'.

By now the Germans were concentrating on bombing London, the battle reaching a most violent crescendo on September 15th. On that day, now celebrated annually as 'Battle of Britain Day', wave after wave of enemy aircraft attacked the capital, being met by 'penny-packet' formations of 11 Group fighters. So great were these attacks, that 11 Group called upon 12 Group for assistance. Douglas Bader sped off from Duxford, his 'Big Wing' arriving over the capital *en masse*. The sight of this mass of RAF fighters new to the fray gave fresh heart to the hard-pressed defenders, but delivered a crushing blow to the enemy aircrews' morale: they had been told that Fighter Command was virtually defeated.

The more fighters are in the air, however, the greater is the quantity of combat claims. This is because the speed of combat frequently deceives the human eye, so several pilots could attack the same enemy aircraft simultaneously, unaware of each other, and each later legitimately claiming to have destroyed a different enemy aircraft. The disparity between losses and claims is now a demonstrable fact, supported by firm and indisputable evidence. Not surprisingly, therefore, post war research has proved that the 'Big Wing' was not actually as successful as was believed at the time. The fact is, however, that the mathematics are irrelevant: here was a huge formation of fighters *being led into battle by a man without legs*!

Many other pilots found the Bader spirit an inspiration. On August 22nd, 1940, for example, Flying Officer Hugh 'Cocky' Dundas of 616 Squadron was shot down over Kent in his Spitfire. When the 20-year old returned to the Squadron from hospital, 616 was contributing aircraft to the 'Big Wing'. Naturally his traumatic experience had somewhat shaken this young pilot's confidence, as Group Captain Sir Hugh Dundas later recalled: -

We were climbing away to the south and the butterflies in my tummy had started to work overtime. Bader's voice then rang out on the radio, calling Woodhall in the Control Room. To my amazement the purpose of his call turned out to be arranging a game of squash! Bader explained to 'Woody' that he had intended to ask a particular person to play with him but had forgotten to do so before taking off. He asked 'Woody' to do it for him. The conversation had a decidedly calming effect on my nerves. It was extraordinary enough that a man without legs should have been thinking about squash in any circumstances. That he should do so whilst leading three squadrons of Hurricanes and two of Spitfires into battle was even more extraordinary. Here, clearly, was a man made in the mould of Nelson and Francis Drake, a man to be followed, a man who would win. I was subsequently to learn, at very close quarters, how true and accurate that first judgement had been.

Inspirational or not, the problem was, however, that the 12 Group 'Big Wing' theory was completely contrary to the established System of Air Defence designed and implemented by the AOC-in-Chief, Air Chief Marshal Sir Hugh Dowding. Whilst the AOC of 11 Group, Air Vice-Marshal Keith Park, complied with the System, but, by permitting 'Big Wing' operations, the AOC 12 Group, Air Vice-Marshal Leigh-Mallory, did not. Nevertheless, Leigh-Mallory, who had never been a fighter pilot (unlike Dowding and Park), was ambitious and keen for his share of accolades and honours when the time came. Whilst Dowding and Park devoted their time and energy to fighting and winning the Battle of Britain, 'LM' used his influence to further support amongst both other officers of air rank and politicians for his Wing tactics. In the back rooms of Whitehall and the House of Commons, therefore, there developed what has been called a 'dirty little intrigue'.

Leigh-Mallory argued that the tactics endorsed by Dowding and Park were too cautious, too conservative, and not sufficiently aggressive. He argued that if large numbers of fighters were

committed to battle, then they would naturally destroy enemy aircraft in like numbers. In support of this argument he produced the 'Big Wing's' *claims*, and his subordinate, Squadron Leader Douglas Bader. Anyone confronted by this charismatic, energetic and enthusiastic dynamo would, I would suggest, find it hard to refuse him anything.

Towards the end of the Battle of Britain, a meeting took place in the Air Council Room of extremely senior RAF officers, mostly of air rank, to discuss the use of Wing formations. It was chaired by Air Vice-Marshal Sholto Douglas, the Deputy Chief of the Air Staff (DCAS), and a friend of Leigh-Mallory's and supporter of the 'Big Wing' theory. The most junior officer present, at whom Dowding looked 'severely', was Squadron Leader Bader, who had been invited by his AOC. It is noteworthy that there were no 11 Group pilots present. Indeed, Dowding and Park had no idea that 12 Group's Douglas Bader had been invited. It soon became apparent, however, that the purpose of the meeting was to push through the use of Wing formations as standard practice, in both attack and defence.

Shortly after the 'Meeting of Infamy', Sholto Douglas replaced Dowding as Commander-in-Chief, and Park was replaced as AOC 11 Group (the most prestigious Group given that it included responsibility for the defence of London) by Leigh-Mallory. This was shameful treatment indeed of the two men who really were the architects of victory in the Battle of Britain. Many years later, Lord Dowding, as he became, learned that even before the Battle of Britain, Leigh-Mallory had stated to Park that he would 'move heaven and earth to get Dowding sacked'. Nevertheless, of Douglas Bader's involvement Dowding wrote: -

I do not think that Bader would ever have allowed himself consciously to become embroiled in such a move. It would probably have come as a shock to him to hear that Leigh-Mallory ever entertained such an idea. It was one thing to disagree with my views, and to express criticisms forcibly, but it was another altogether to intrigue against his own Commander-in-Chief, which is why I think the latter was out of the question.

It is my belief that although the record proves Dowding and Park's tactics correct, Douglas Bader was merely trying to push through tactics that he wholeheartedly believed were right in our nation's hour of need. As Douglas himself said later: -

There have been some appalling books written on this subject, which malign me tremendously, saying that I had done my best to torpedo Dowding and Park. It is absurd, in fact, to suggest that a mere Acting Squadron Leader would have such power and influence. Some of the authors concerned should have known better.

By the autumn of 1940, the German bomber force was unable to sustain such heavy losses over England by day. So began the terrible night *blitz*, but with this change in tactics and the worsening weather, the chance of invading England, that year at least, was over. Had Fighter Command not held out throughout that Indian summer, the Germans would have marched up Whitehall. Let there be no mistake about that, and neither should there be ambiguity regarding Hitler's intention, which was to make Britain a slave market for the Nazi empire. The debt we owe to Churchill's fabled 'Few' will always, therefore, remain immeasurable.

On October 1st, 1940, Squadron Leader Bader was awarded the Distinguished Service Order. This decoration is awarded essentially for outstanding leadership, and there can be no doubt that this was Douglas Bader's greatest contribution. Under his command, 242 Squadron had been transformed

from a demoralised unit to a top fighter squadron possessed of only the highest morale. Air Marshal Sir Denis Crowley-Milling was a young Pilot Officer in 1940, and remembered that: -

Less than a month after he took command of the Squadron, morale was very high. Fear was ever present, of course, but Bader was afraid of nothing and through both example and constant encouragement he helped us all conquer our own anxieties. You always felt perfectly safe when flying with Douglas Bader. For me, his arrival at Coltishall was the start of 18 exciting months of operational flying together, an unforgettable experience that helped shape my subsequent career.

Understandably, the propaganda machine made much of Bader's exploits, which had all the ingredients of a massive morale-boosting story. The story inspired the nation. Even a small provincial newspaper, the *Malvern Gazette*, included the following reference to the incident in an article entitled 'The Extra Bit', aimed at encouraging donations to the town's 'Spitfire Fund': -

Remember the story of the young pilot who lost his legs in a crash? Fitted with artificial legs he argued his way back into the RAF; argued his way through the medical boards; argued his way into a squadron, and one day, quite recently, he went up alone and shot a Dornier down into the sea. Did he say 'I've given the country my legs; why should I now be expected to give them my neck?' Not a bit! Like all those gallant lads he was ready to give the extra. God bless them for it.

Douglas Bader was already a legend within the RAF, and justifiably so given his sporting and aerobatic achievements, not to mention returning to successfully command a fighter squadron without legs. The media now projected this beyond just the service, and forevermore Douglas Bader became the most famous pilot who not only fought in the Battle of Britain, but throughout the whole war. Indeed, many years later, a certain television presenter introduced him as 'the leader of Churchill's Few during the Battle of Britain'! Some took exception. Wing Commander HR 'Dizzy' Allen: -

I am constantly bemused why Group Captain Sir Douglas Bader and the Battle of Britain should be considered synonymous. If he had served in the front line of No 11 Group, based essentially in Kent and Sussex, he might have realised that the 'Big Wing' concept was balderdash, for the front line anyway – and that was the line that mattered.

This is not to denigrate Douglas Bader's sheer determination in getting himself back into the RAF with tin legs, nor his distinguished record on the later fighter sweeps over France. But I do wish that he would not allow himself to be pressed continually as the epitome of the Battle of Britain pilot. That is not his place in history, but he carved his own niche elsewhere.

Perhaps, however, his critics have never considered that Douglas Bader himself had no control over the media and what journalists chose to say about him. He recorded his own views on the Battle of Britain in writing on January 2nd, 1968; these previously unpublished notes are reproduced below: -

It is difficult for someone who was privileged to fight in the Battle of Britain to write about it. Like many other battles in history it became important only in retrospect to those who fought it. The Prime Minister, the War Cabinet, the Commander-in-Chief of Fighter Command all knew without doubt what was at stake. The pilots, however, certainly did not.

They were a good bunch, these pilots – young, light-hearted, prone to understatement in order to hide their feelings. They coined a new slang appropriate to the event, some of which has now become part of the English language. They took a dim view of those German warplanes with their iron crosses and their crooked swastikas flying over our island kingdom and dropping bombs. We learned to hate, though not so much as the few Czechs and Poles fighting with us who knew the uncivilised savagery of the Hun occupation of their homelands.

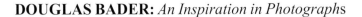

Memories of those tremendous days of August and September 1940, are kaleidoscopic. Two Hurricanes converging on the same *Junkers* 88. You cannot shout a warning because there is no common radio frequency. The Hurricanes touch, a wing breaks off and floats away like a falling leaf. One pilot bales out and lands safely to continue the fight another day. You are closing on a *Dornier* 17 when some sixth sense makes you look up to see a Spitfire diving vertically from above. As you sheer away the Spitfire hits the *Dornier* fair and square. It wraps itself round the fighter and they both go down on fire and seemingly quite slowly – like a ball of paper that has been set alight and thrown into the air. A stream of bullets crashes into the dashboard of your Hurricane and you nearly die of fright as you wrench it round. You see the *Messerschmitt* that nearly got you go past in an ever-steepening dive with the Hurricane on its tail that has killed it. As you watch, the *Messerschmitt* disappears into the pall of smoke from the burning oil tanks at Shell Haven on the north bank of the Thames Estuary. Of such are the memories that can still stir the blood 29 years later.

The fighter pilot's pattern of life during the high summer of 1940, was readiness from dawn to dusk. Long hours, boring hours, hell on the digestion, interspersed with moments of tremendous exhilaration. You sat around the airfield near your aeroplanes, playing cards, gossiping, reading magazines, playing the gramophone; meals were brought out. You were just finishing lunch when the alarm went. As you climbed away into the blue sky you thought that the coffee would be cold when you got back, should you order some more or should you wait until teatime. When you got back you decided to wait until teatime but the same thing happened. None of us who were lucky enough to be there would exchange the experience for anything else in life. We fighter pilots were over-praised by the great Winston Churchill's superlative and now historic phrase about the 'Few'. We loved him for it and remain lastingly proud.

Nevertheless we knew then, and with more certainty afterwards, that every man and woman in these islands won the Battle of Britain. We were the lucky ones who could fight back whilst others on the ground had no choice but to take it – the incendiary and high explosive bombs and all that went with them. Men and women serviced and repaired our Hurricanes and Spitfires and built us more; industry continued to work. The gallant merchant seamen escorted by the Royal Navy brought to our shores food and fuel and much else which sustained life. The fighter pilots were their countrymen's representatives in the air. The real enduring memory is of a united British people from all Four Corners of the earth.

Douglas Bader himself realised that the public interest in him did not arise alone from him being a famous and successful fighter pilot. By his own admission there were many pilots with either equal or greater ability than he, but who never received public recognition and acclaim. The fact of the matter was that people were inspired by Douglas mastering his disability to the extent that he went on to fly in action.

Considering the Battle of Britain as a backdrop, the following story from William Walker, himself one of the Few, provides a glimpse of the real Bader:-

On August 26th, 1940, I was shot down and baled out of my Spitfire, wounded. Having landed in the Channel I was fortunately rescued and eventually ended up in the RAF Hospital at Halton. On our ward was a youngster of about 17, as I recall, whose leg was about to be amputated. He was dreadfully upset, but one day, before the operation, Douglas Bader came to see him. In straightforward terms he told the youngster that he must not allow this misfortune to affect him so negatively, and that he must get on with it and fight back. Given that Bader, an Acting Squadron Leader and CO of a fighter squadron, was a double amputee must have been inspiring to the boy.

But for Douglas Bader himself the war continued. Early in 1941, it was decided to organise Fighter Command into Wings, each comprising three squadrons and based at Sector Stations. A new post was therefore created: 'Wing Commander Flying'. As the name implies, the post was an operational rather than an administrative one. Not surprisingly, Douglas Bader, who by this time had added a Distinguished Flying Cross to his existing DSO, was amongst the first Wing Leaders appointed.

Considering Biggin Hill too close to London's social distractions, he chose Tangmere, near Chichester on the south coast.

On March 18th, 1941, Wing Commander Douglas Bader DSO DFC, reported to RAF Tangmere's Station Commander and took up his new appointment. Sir Alan Smith remembers that day vividly:

Sitting in readiness at dispersal I heard the roar of a Spitfire as it dived low, climbed, did a half-roll and lowered its undercarriage whilst inverted, rolled out, side-slipped and made a perfect landing. Out of the cockpit climbed Wing Commander Douglas Bader and he walked with his distinctive gait into dispersal.

The Wing Commander announced himself, said he would be leading the Tangmere Wing and explained that he would do so with 616 Squadron. He obviously knew Flying Officer 'Cocky' Dundas and Pilot Officer 'Johnnie' Johnson, and said "You'll be Red 3, 'Cocky', and you 'Johnnie' will be Red 4." Looking around he caught my eye and said, "Who are you?"

"Sergeant Smith, Sir", I replied.

"Right, you fly as my Red 2 and God help you if you don't watch my tail!"

I couldn't believe my ears, it was like God asking me to keep an eye on heaven for him! Flying with Douglas, 'Cocky' and 'Johnnie' was to become the greatest experience of my life and I considered myself quite the most fortunate Sergeant pilot in the RAF.

Squadron Leader LH 'Buck' Casson also remembers Wing Commander Bader during the spring of 1941: -

I had first met him at Coltishall on September 3rd, 1940, when he tried to tick some of us off for having our top buttons undone in true fighter pilot's style. I came to know him briefly during early 1941, when we occasionally joined up with 242 Squadron as a 12 Group Wing flying from either Duxford or Wittering. Of course I came to know him much better at Tangmere from March 1941 onwards. We enjoyed playing golf with Douglas at Goodwood, and at the house where he was billeted with his wife, Thelma, the "Bay House" (known by the pilots as the "Bag House") near Bognor, we carried him to the pool where he swam extremely well. He always wanted company so we often went to his digs for a drink and a chat.

Flight Lieutenant William Walker:-

Upon discharge from hospital and being declared fit, I returned to 616 Squadron which was then at Westhampnett and a part of Douglas Bader's new Tangmere Wing. To pass the time we often played table tennis, and Douglas would never give up. He would insist on playing on and on until he won, as he just could not bear to be beaten by anything. Douglas and his wife, Thelma, had moved to live near the airfield at the 'Bayhouse'. Once when I was there with some other pilots she asked us not to play table tennis with Douglas he afterwards he would arrive home in agony with his stumps rubbed raw by the exertion. Extraordinary.

Sergeant Bob 'Butch' Morton remembers: -

At Tangmere we were joined by Wing Commander Bader, who was already something of a legend. My first sight of him was sitting on the radiator of Billy Burton's car holding a shotgun, whilst the CO drove him erratically across the field in pursuit of rabbits!

At this time I had a coat of arms painted on my Mae West: argent, on a pale azure, three crowns for Hull, on a chief of the second the tail of a Spitfire diving into a cloud; the motto was "Spotto, Squirto, Scrammo", or I spot, I squirt,

I remove myself. It was highly commended by Wing Commander Bader!

The intention was for Fighter Command to go over to the offensive in 1941, 'Leaning into France' and taking the war to the Germans. By employing wings of fighters, the expectation was that the *Luftwaffe* would be destroyed *en masse*. During the Battle of Britain, however, RAF controllers had learned not to respond to pure fighter sweeps, the point being that fighters can only inflict damage if engaged. To force the RAF to join battle, therefore, the Germans included fighter-bombers in their formations, meaning that they could not be ignored. Fighter Command was to find the same thing in 1941; fighter sweeps were largely ignored, and 'Rhubarbs', being nuisance raids by pairs of Spitfires, achieved little when offset against the losses involved. So was born the 'Circus'. In this operation, various fighter wings would escort a small number of medium bombers to attack industrial and military targets in France. This meant that the defending German fighters had to react. The theory was that when they did, large numbers of hungry Spitfires would be awaiting them. Keen, aggressive leaders like Douglas Bader were therefore ideal for this so-called 'Non-Stop Offensive'. The Tangmere Wing would soon find itself heavily engaged in these cross-Channel raids.

At Westhampnett appeared a notice: -

BADER'S BUS COMPANY
Daily trips to the Continent
<u>RETURN TICKETS ONLY!</u>

Throughout this time, Sergeant Alan Smith flew regularly in 'Dogsbody Section' as Wing Commander Bader's Red Two. He recalls: -

Whenever we flew over France on fighter sweeps or escorting bombers, we were always the last to return to base. Mission completed and everyone else going home, Douglas would hang around looking for a Hun to engage so long as we had ammunition and enough fuel to get us back to base.

As soon as we crossed over the English coast, Douglas would slide back his cockpit cover, and out would come his pipe which he lit and puffed away upon contentedly. I could not help reflecting that he was virtually sitting on his petrol tank!

'Johnnie' Johnson too remembered the Wing Leader smoking whilst piloting a volatile combination of fuel and ammunition: -

Oh yes, he used to light a match in the cockpit, 'Swan Vestas', he'd be there puffing away, we couldn't see him for smoke sometimes!

Smoking aboard His Majesty's aircraft was not only strictly forbidden, it was also extremely dangerous! However, in Wing Commander Bader's case this only served to enhance the growing myth that he was indestructible. Even his wife, Thelma, living at the Bay House with her sister, Jill, came to believe wholeheartedly that the Germans would never get Douglas. When he returned from a sortie over France, Spitfire 'DB' would swoop low overhead. At night, however, Wing Commander Bader slept at Tangmere in the Officers' Mess, 'just to keep in touch'.

As Douglas Bader had already led 616 Squadron in the air as a part of his Duxford Wing, he chose

to lead the Tangmere Wing at this squadron's head. Consequently, Squadron Leader Burton, 616 Squadron's CO, was to become the Wing Leader's right-hand man. Burton's 21-year-old wife, Jean, was a 'camp follower'. Now Mrs Jean Allom, she remembers: -

Douglas and Billy were great friends despite the gap in age and seniority, but no doubt their mutual Cranwell background played a part in this. On May 9th, 1941, 616 moved to Westhampnett (now Goodwood racecourse). I had spent a very cold and snowy winter up at Kirton and so was delighted to be back in warmer climes and to find lodgings in a large country house in Lavant; from the bottom of the garden I had a ringside seat of the squadron taking-off and landing. I could thus approximately gauge the time 616 would return from a sweep and station myself in the garden anxiously and hopefully to await the return of Billy's Spitfire, 'QJ-K'. Although this was to prove a somewhat stressful occupation, the relief when I saw the familiar aircraft letters landing was more than worth it.

I had already met Douglas Bader and his first wife, Thelma, the previous summer in Norfolk, but during 1941, got to know them really well, largely due to their generous open-house entertaining at the Bay House. In the evenings Billy and I, together with other members of the Wing, were often invited. It was a friendship that lasted until the Baders' deaths and one that I valued greatly.

Air Vice-Marshal 'Johnnie' Johnson recalls his early impressions of Douglas Bader: -

I suppose it was fairly awe-inspiring really, we were Pilot Officers and so on and he was older, Wing Commander DSO DFC, legendary, but he treated us all as equals, he was a great leader. Of course we faced that summer with the prospect of a renewed Battle of Britain type bombardment, but Douglas would rub his hands together and say "Let the buggers come across, we've got the Wing and the cannon now, bloody good show old boy, and if they don't come then we'll go over there, won't we?" To say that he was enthusiastic was an understatement! He'd come stumping into dispersal and say to Billy Burton, "What are we doing today then Billy?", and Billy might respond, "Well the Form 'D' (Operational Order) has come through, Sir, but we're not on it, the other Wings are but not us". Bader would say, "Right, we'll see about that, I'll have a bloody word with L.M.!". And then he would ring the AOC and, lo and behold, we would be on Ops!

Aside from the awesome reputation Wing Commander Bader was clearly developing as leader of the Tangmere Wing, Harry Jacks, an Administration Clerk, caught a glimpse of the great man's humanitarian side: -

During one of the rare moments when Wing Commander Bader discussed personal matters with me, he learned of the serious health problems of my widowed mother. He urged me to apply for a compassionate posting back to 610's home station, Hooton Park. Members of the Auxiliary Air Force could not be posted away from their squadron unless they signed a 'Certificate of Willingness to be Posted', which I consequently did. Wing Commander Bader appended a strong recommendation to my application. My posting came through, subject to my having signed the said certificate, and so back near home I went.

Harry also remembers the 'Bader Factor': -

There were a couple of events which caused Wing Commander Bader to blow his 'stack' and use very strong language to senior officers at Group HQ. On one occasion a signal was received ordering the Wing Commander to exchange his Vauxhall staff car for a smaller 8 hp model, and, second, another signal arrived ordering him to return to Group inventory one of his two aircraft, either his black-painted night-flying Hurricane, or his Spitfire. It is my recollection that neither instruction was acted upon!

Sergeant Frank Twitchett, a pilot in the Tangmere Wing's 145 Squadron: -

In 1941, we also began to do Channel sweeps, although these were largely ineffective, as they were purely fighter

operations and the *Luftwaffe* very sensibly remained on the ground not intercepting aircraft which posed no threat unless engaged. In March, Wing Commander Bader had arrived, and by April things were really starting to happen. Throughout May 1941, we undertook several sorties up and down the Channel attempting to flush out some opposition. In June 1941, with the Wing in position and with 145 Squadron now established at Merston, whilst both 616 and 610 were based at Westhampnett, the sweeps started in earnest and we often swept to Dunkirk, Calais, Boulogne, usually taking Blenheims. On one occasion, June 18th, we even took three Stirlings. Later, the Forêt de Licques was bombed and on this occasion we lost Sergeants Turnbull and Palmer. The average per pilot was two sweeps daily, and this, you can appreciate, became a little wearing on the nerves. We flew to such targets as Lille, Hazebrouck, Béthune, Le Touquet, St Omer, and even one to Knocke on the Belgian coast. That was particularly worrying as we escorted six Blenheims to bomb an oil tanker which had anchored just off the coast and was covered by six flak ships. Four of the six Blenheims were lost and two squadrons of Me 109s attacked us. The whole operation and dogfight took place only about 500 feet above the sea!

The feeling that we were going onto the offensive ourselves gave everyone a great fillip in the sense that we had finished having our backs to the wall and were finally going to deal out some of the punishment which we felt Jerry richly deserved. Perhaps if we had looked forward to the enormous efforts of the couple of years following 1941, we might have seen life a little differently. A very good friend of mine once summed up the Non-stop Offensive by saying that at that point in time we were sure that we would win the war, but were not sure how; sooner or later we would prevail and emerge victorious. Fortunately for us his prophecy came true.

During the Battle of Britain, Duxford's Station Commander and Chief Controller was Wing Commander AB Woodhall. Bader and 'Woody' had developed quite a rapport during 1940. The latter, a former RFC pilot in the Great War, not only supported his subordinate's Big Wing theory but also that of allowing the leader in the air to make many of his own decisions, as opposed to being inflexibly tied to instructions from the ground. 'Woody' established a special bond of understanding between himself, on the ground, and those in the air, as not all controllers were able. In April 1941, this partnership resumed when Group Captain Woodhall became Station Commander of RAF Tangmere, a posting and promotion no doubt engineered by Air Vice-Marshal Leigh-Mallory who wanted his old team back together again.

The Tangmere Wing's radio callsign became 'Greenline Bus', from which the unofficial 'Bader's Bus Company' was derived. Tangmere Control became 'Beetle'. Bader was to operate his squadrons in a fashion similar to Duxford days: there was no forming up over the airfield, squadrons would slot into their allocated positions as the Wing progressed outbound. The usual practice would then be for the Wing to rendezvous with bombers over Beachy Head, codenamed 'Diamond'. Flight Lieutenant Ron Rayner recalled those days: -

There would be this mass of Spitfires orbiting Beachy Head, going round and round in circles over the English coast until everyone was together. Then Bader would say "Okay, we're going" and the Beehive would then proceed across the Channel to France.

In the Tangmere Operations Room were WAAF plotters, the 'Beauty Chorus', who pushed counters representing the squadrons across a map of southern England and northern France. A tannoy system enabled them to share the action when battle was joined. However, on occasions Group Captain Woodhall felt obliged to turn off the sound! Amongst the offenders was Wing Commander Bader, as Johnnie Johnson recalls: -

Well Douglas was very 'salty', you know, always 'effing and blinding. Woodhall would shout up and say "Come on, Douglas, I've got WAAFs down here," and Bader would just reply, "Oh its all right, I'll come and see 'em and apologise!"

The combats taking place high over France were often fast, furious and lethal, as illustrated by Wing Commander Bader's report of a combat on July 2ⁿᵈ, 1941: -

I was leading 616 Squadron's first section. Sighted approximately 15 Me 109Fs a few miles SW of Lille, so turned south and attacked them. They were in a sort of four formation climbing eastwards. They made no attempt to do anything but climb in formation so I turned the squadron behind them and attacked from about 200 feet above and behind. I attacked an Me 109F from quarter astern to astern, and saw his hood come off - he probably jettisoned it - and the pilot started to climb out. Did not see him actually bale out as I nearly collided with another Me 109 that was passing on my right in the middle of a half-roll. Half-rolled with him and dived down on his tail, firing at him with the result that glycol and oil came out of his machine. I left him at about 12000', as he appeared determined to continue diving, and pulled up again to 18,000 feet. My ASI showed rather more than 400 mph when I pulled out. Found the fight had taken me west a bit so picked up two 610 Squadron Spitfires and flew out at Boulogne, round Griz-Nez and up to Gravelines where we crossed the coast again and found an Me 109E at 8,000 feet, and at which I fired from about 300 yards. No damage, but this one is claimed as "Frightened"! The first 109 is claimed as destroyed since, although I did not actually see the pilot leave the aircraft, I saw him preparing to do so, and several pilots of 616 saw two parachutes going down, the pilot of one of which was shot down by Pilot Officer Hepple. The second 109 was seen by Pilot Officer Hepple and is claimed as damaged.

On this day, Wing Commander DRS Bader DSO DFC was awarded a Bar to the DSO, and Squadron Leader Holden a DFC.

Two days later the Wing Commander recorded another combat success: -

Intercepted one Me 109E some miles south of Gravelines at 14,000 feet, while with a section of four. Turned onto its tail and opened fire with a short, 1 second burst at about 150 yards. I found it very easy to keep inside him during the turn and closed quite quickly. I gave him three more short bursts, the final one at about 20 yards range; as he slowed down very suddenly I nearly collided with him. I did not see the result except one puff of smoke half way through. Squadron Leader Burton in my section watched the complete combat and saw the Me 109's airscrew slow right down to ticking over speed. As I broke away, the 109 did not half-roll and dive, but just sort of fell away in a sloppy fashion, quite slowly, as though the pilot had been hit. Having broken away, I did not see the 109 I attacked, since I was trying to collect my section together. I am, however, satisfied that I was hitting him and so is squadron Leader Burton, from whose evidence this report is written.

Wing Commander Bader's victim was *Leutnant* Joachim Kehrhahn of I/JG26. He was killed when his Me 109E-7 (6476) crashed at St Pol.

Again, however, Douglas was looking at tactics, but as they related to actual fighter-to-fighter combat. Johnnie Johnson: -

The RAF version of the 'Finger Four' was really Cocky Dundas' idea. We had all seen the Germans flying in these loose formations. In 1941 we could see these *Schwarms* of German fighters, lean and hungry looking with plenty of room between them. Our training, however, was quite disgusting. I remember flying on September 15th, 1940, climbing up to the south when my section leader said "You're too far out", and my wing was overlapping his at the time! The idea of the "vic", of course, was that we all manoeuvred as one, 24 machine-guns firing together. It was disgusting, and because of our antiquated tactics a terrible number of young chaps were to be slaughtered without even knowing what had hit them because they were concentrating intently upon tight formation flying. That was even towards the end of the Battle of Britain. Astonishing.

Prior to going to Tangmere, we of 616 Squadron were not flying "vics" but in pairs. I remember that in the autumn of 1940, Dundas and I were scrambled together from Kirton, just a pair of us flying out, covering each other like a pair of hunting dogs. When we got to Tangmere, we were told that we were going to fly three fours in line astern. Sometimes they put a pair of weavers over the squadron but these were often never seen again, being the first to be

picked off. Then Bader arrived and at first we flew in the three fours, the loose fours being in line astern, but then Dundas, who of course had already been shot down, suggested that we should fly the fours in line abreast. Consequently, after a little experimentation, we adopted this in May 1941. Prior to that, there was no tactical training, no one ever taught me how to get on the tail of a 109. Bader was the first man who started to talk to us about tactics. He had the ability to dissect an air battle and learn from it.

Despite his enthusiastic and confident aura, however, Wing Commander Bader was not superhuman. He, like Fighter Command's other Wing Leaders, was becoming exhausted. Nevertheless, as the reader would expect of this great and forthright man, he pressed on, very much regardless.

By this time, Nazi Germany had invaded Soviet Russia, thus turning its territorial ambitions eastward. The Russians now turned to the Allies for help and clamoured for the opening of a second front. Britain, however and remembering that America was still neutral, was in no position to launch the liberation of Occupied Europe. Air operations were, therefore, the British government's only means of demonstrating positive support for Russia. It was hoped that by keeping up the pressure, the *Luftwaffe* would be forced to return units westwards to defend the Channel coast. Despite the demonstrable bravery of the Allied pilots, this would ultimately prove a forlorn hope. Furthermore, as there were no targets in Northern France capable of crippling the German war machine, the enemy fighter pilots were able to choose carefully when and where they attacked the RAF formations. Being used in its intended (defensive) role, the Me 109 came into its own. The RAF fighters, often operating at the extremity of their range and contending with two sea crossings, faced a reversal of the Battle of Britain situation. Although morale throughout Fighter Command was high, so too were losses. Fighter Command was losing many experienced pilots and leaders over France; to the Germans, the 'Non-Stop Offensive' became known as the 'Non-sense Offensive'.

On the morning of Monday, August 9th, 1941, the teleprinter clattered away at Tangmere as the Form 'D' came through from 11 Group HQ detailing the Tangmere Wing's task for the day. This was to be another complex Circus, No 68, involving many aircraft to Gosnay. The Tangmere Wing was to provide Target Support.

Sergeant Alan Smith, Wing Commander Bader's usual 'Dogsbody 2', had a head cold and so was unable to fly. His place was taken by the New Zealander, Sergeant Jeff West, a pilot with one-and-a-half Me 109s destroyed and one damaged to his credit.

For this Target Support sortie to Gosnay, 'Dogsbody' Section therefore consisted of: -

Dogsbody: Wing Commander Douglas Bader DSO* DFC.
Dogsbody 2:   Sergeant Jeff West.
Dogsbody 3:   Flight Lieutenant Hugh Dundas DFC.
Dogsbody 4:   Pilot Officer 'Johnnie' Johnson.

Take-off came at 1040 hrs, 'Dogsbody' Section leading Westhampnett's Spitfires for yet another sortie into very hostile airspace. High over Chichester, Squadron Leader Holden swiftly manoeuvred 610 Squadron into position above and slightly to port of 616. As the Wing was Target Support, it had no bombers to meet prior to setting course for France, although the Spitfires were still routed out over Beachy Head. As the Wing left Chichester, however, there was no sign of 41 Squadron (the

Wing now comprised 616, 610 and 41 Squadrons).

For some reason, 41 Squadron missed the rendezvous so, unable to wait, 616 and 610 Squadrons set course for France, adopting their battle formations in the process. Still climbing, Wing Commander Bader waggled his wings insistently, indicating that 'Dogsbody 3', Flight Lieutenant Dundas, should take the lead. Dundas slid across, tucking his wing tip just two or three feet from Bader's. From this close proximity, Dundas saw the Wing Leader mouth two words: 'Airspeed Indicator', meaning that the instrument on W3185 was u/s. The Wing had to climb at the right speed to arrive over the target at the appointed time, which was crucial. Dundas gave a 'thumbs up' and moved forward to lead the Spitfires to France. On the rear of his hand he had fortunately written the time at which the Wing was due over the French coast in addition to the speed which had to be maintained. The 21-year-old flight commander then 'settled down to concentrate on the job'.

The Spitfires cruised over the Channel and towards France with 610 Squadron above and behind 616. Dundas led the Wing over the French coast right on cue This crucial timing observed, Bader accelerated ahead and informed 'Dogsbody 3' over the R/T that he was resuming the lead. The Spitfires' arrival over the coastal *flak* belt was greeted by dangerous little puffballs of black smoke that made the formation twist and turn. 'Beetle' then called 'Dogsbody' informing that the beehive itself was 'on time and engaged'. As the Spitfires forged inland, therefore, some distance behind them the bombers and various cover Wings were now bound for France and action.

Slightly below the condensation trail level, a 610 Squadron pilot reported seeing contrails 'above and to our left'. Squadron Leader Holden consequently led the squadron higher still whilst 'Beetle' (B) reported: -

B: 'Dogsbody from Beetle. There are 20 plus five miles to the east of you.'
DB: 'OK, but your transmitter is quite impossible. Please use the other.'
B: 'Dogsbody is this better?'
DB: 'Perfect. Ken, start getting more height'.
KH: 'OK, Dogsbody, but will you throttle back? I cannot keep up'.
DB: 'Sorry Ken, my airspeed indicator is u/s. Throttling back, and I will do one slow
        left-hand turn so you can catch up.'
KH: 'Dogsbody from Ken, I'm making "smoke" at this height.'
DB: 'OK, Ken, I'm going down very slightly.'

'Beetle' then advised 'Dogsbody' of more bandits in the vicinity. 616 Squadron's Flying Officer Roy Marples (RM) saw the enemy first: 'Three bandits coming down astern of us. I'm keeping an eye on them, now there are six.'

DB: 'OK'.
B: 'Douglas, another 12 plus ahead and slightly higher.'
RM: 'Eleven of them now'.
DB: 'OK, Roy, let me know exactly where they are.'
RM: 'About one mile astern and slightly higher'.
B: 'Douglas, there is another 40 plus 15 miles to the north-east of you.'
DB: 'OK Beetle. Are our friends where they ought to be, I haven't much idea where I am.'
B: 'Yes, you are exactly right. And so are your friends.'
RM: 'Dogsbody from Roy. Keep turning left and you'll see 109s at nine o'clock.'

DB: 'Ken, can you see them?'
KH: 'Douglas, 109s below. Climbing up'.

By this time, 616 and 610 Squadrons had progressed into a very dangerous French sky indeed, Beetle having already reported some 72 bandits, representing odds outnumbering the Spitfires by nearly 3:1. Clearly this was not to be an uneventful sortie. Apprehension mounting, the Spitfire pilots switched on their gunsight reflectors and gun buttons to 'fire'. Anxiously the sky was searched, an ever-watchful eye being kept on the 109s positioned 1,000 feet above the Wing and waiting to pounce. Bader himself dipped each wing in turn, scrutinising the sky below for the 109s reported by Ken Holden.

DB: 'I can't see them, will you tell me where to look?'
KH: 'Underneath Bill's section now. Shall I come down?'
DB: 'No, I have them. Get into formation. Going down. Ken, are you with us?'
KH: 'Just above you'.

As Dogsbody Section dived on the enemy, Flight Lieutenant Casson followed with three other aircraft of 'B' Flight.

'Dogsbody 3', Flight Lieutenant Dundas, had 'smelt a rat' in respect of the *Schwarm* of 109s that Dogsbody Section was now rapidly diving towards. Finding no targets to the Section's right, 'Dogsbody 4', Pilot Officer Johnson, skidded under the section and fired at an Me 109 on the left. By this time the whole of Dogsbody Section was firing, although Dundas, still unhappy and suspecting a trap, had a compelling urge to look behind. Suddenly Pilot Officer Hepple shouted over the R/T:-

'Blue 2 here. Some buggers coming down behind, astern. Break left!'

The Spitfire pilots hauled their aircraft around in steep turns. The sky behind Dogsbody Section was full of Me 109s, all firing - without Hepple's warning the Spitfires would have been 'nailed'. As the high 109s crashed into 616 Squadron, Squadron Leader Holden decided that it was time for his section to join the fray and reduce the odds. Informing Flight Lieutenant Denis Crowley-Milling of this decision, Holden led his Spitfires down to assist. 'Buck' Casson, following Bader's Section, was well throttled back to keep his flight together. Also attacking from the rear, Casson managed a squirt at a *Rotte* of 109s. Flying Officer Marples, No 3 in Casson's section, then shouted a warning of even more 109s diving upon the Wing, whilst Squadron Leader Billy Burton urged the Spitfires to 'Keep turning', thus preventing the 109s (which could not out-turn a Spitfire), getting in a shot. Suddenly the organised chaos became a totally confused maelstrom of twisting, turning fighters.

Johnnie Johnson remembers: -

There was this scream of "Break!" - and we all broke, we didn't wait to hear it twice! Round, then a swirling mass of 109s and Spitfires. When I broke I could see Bader still firing. Dundas was firing at the extreme right 109. There was some cloud nearby and I disappeared into it as quick as possible! I couldn't say how many aircraft were involved, suffice to say a lot. It seemed to me that the greatest danger was a collision, rather than being shot down, that's how close we all were. We had got the 109s we were bouncing and then Holden came down with his section, so there were a lot of aeroplanes. We were fighting 109Fs, although there may have been some Es amongst them. There was an absolute mass of aeroplanes just 50 yards apart, it was awful. I thought to myself "You're going to collide with

somebody!" I didn't think about shooting at anything after we were bounced ourselves, all you could think about was surviving, getting out of that mass of aircraft. In such a tight turn, of course, you almost black out, you cannot really see where you are going. It was a mess. I had never been so frightened in my life, never!

Chased by three Me 109s, the closest just 100 yards astern, Pilot Officer Johnson maintained his tight turn, spiralling down towards the safety of a nearby cloud which his Spitfire dived into with over 400 mph on the clock. Pulling back the throttle and centralising the controls, the altimeter stabilised, but, speed having dropped to less than 100 mph, the Spitfire stalled. Beneath the cloud, 'Dogsbody 4' recovered control. Having requested and received a homing course for Dover, he headed rapidly for England. Over the R/T, Pilot Officer Johnson could still hear 616 and 610 Squadrons' running battle: -

'Get into formation or they'll shoot the bloody lot of you!'
'Spitfire going down in flames, 10 o'clock.'
'YQ-C (616 Squadron Spitfire). Form up on me, I'm at three o'clock to you.'
'Four buggers above us', from "Nip" Hepple.
'All Elfin aircraft (616 Squadron) withdraw. I say again, all Elfin aircraft withdraw.'
'Use the cloud if you're in trouble', from "Billy" Burton.
'Are you going home, Ken?', also from Burton.
'Yes, withdrawing', from Holden.
'Ken from Crow. Are you still about?'
'I'm right behind you, Crow'.
'Are we all here?'
'Two short.'
' Dogsbody from Beetle. Do you require any assistance?'
'Beetle from Elfin Leader. We are OK and withdrawing.'
'Thank you Billy. Douglas, do you require any assistance? Steer three four zero to the coast.'

The silence from 'Dogsbody' was ominous.

Returning to the French coast, Pilot Officer Johnson saw a lone Me 109 below. Suspecting it to be one of the three which chased him into the cloud just a few minutes previously, 'Johnnie' anxiously searched the sky for the other two: the sky was clear. From astern, 'Dogsbody 4' dropped below the 109 before attacking from its blind spot, below and behind. One burst of cannon shells sent the enemy fighter diving earthwards emitting a plume of black smoke.

Pilot Officer Johnson came 'out of France on the deck, low and fast', his Spitfire roaring over waving peasants, just feet above their fields. At the coast, German soldiers ran to their guns, but in a second the fleeting Spitfire was gone. Climbing over the Channel, 'Dogsbody 4' realised that something might have happened to Wing Commander Bader: -

As I was crossing the Channel, Woodhall, who obviously knew that there had been a fight from the radar and R/T, repeated "Douglas, are you receiving?" This came over the air every five minutes or so. I therefore called up and said "Its 'Johnnie' here Sir, we've had a stiff fight and I last saw the Wing Commander on the tail of a 109".' He said, "Thank you, I'll meet you at dispersal".

The silence from 'Dogsbody' over the R/T clearly meant one of two things, either that his radio was u/s, or he had somehow been brought down. Air Marshal Sir Denis Crowley-Milling, then a flight commander in Ken Holden's 610 Squadron, recalls that 'the greatest impression I have of August

9th, 1941, is the silence on the R/T. Douglas always maintained a running commentary. Had the worst happened?'

So confused had been the fighting, so numerous the aircraft in this incredible maelstrom over St Omer, that only Wing Commander Bader himself had the answers to the questions regarding his present state and whereabouts. After the first charge, 'Dogsbody' had found himself alone after flattening out at 24,000 feet. In front of him were six 109s flying in a line abreast formation of three pairs. Flying alone, Bader knew that he should leave this enemy formation and adhere to the instructions which he had even issued to his pilots as formal instructions: get out and get home. He considered that these 109s were 'sitters'; in a split second, greed won over discipline and good judgement: alone over France, Wing Commander Bader stalked the middle *Rotte*. He later reported: -

I saw some more Me 109s. I arrived amongst these, who were evidently not on the lookout, as I expect they imagined the first formation we attacked to be covering them. I got a very easy shot at one of these which flew quite straight until he went on fire from behind the cockpit - a burst of about three seconds.

As two 109s curved towards him, 'Dogsbody' broke right, violently, although anticipating, with some bravado, that his course would take him between a pair of 109s. Suddenly something hit Spitfire 'DB'. Due to the close proximity of the enemy aircraft, Bader assumed that he had collided with a 109. The Spitfire went completely out of control, diving earthwards, its control column limp and unresponsive. As he looked behind, Bader's impression was that the entire fuselage aft of the VHF aerial had disappeared, although he was later to report that it was 'probably just the empennage'.

At 24,000 feet, 'Dogsbody' was unable to consider escape due to the lack of oxygen outside the cockpit at that height. His dilemma, however, was that the doomed fighter was already travelling in excess of 400 mph, so would soon be subjected to forces so great that baling out would in any case be impossible. Yanking the canopy release mechanism, the hood was sucked away, the cockpit immediately being battered by the airflow. Without legs though, would he be able to thrust his body upward to get out? As he struggled to get his head above the windscreen, he was nearly plucked out of the cockpit, but half way he became stuck - the rigid foot of his artificial right leg jamming in the cockpit, the grip vice-like. Ever downwards the fighter plunged, the pilot helpless and continuously battered by the rushing wind, half in and half out of his crashing aeroplane. Desperately gripping his parachute's 'D' ring, Douglas Bader struggled furiously to get out. Eventually, at about 6,000 feet, the offending artificial leg's restraining strap broke. Free at last, the pilot was plucked out into mid-air; as the Spitfire continued its dive, he experienced a moment of apparently floating upwards. That terrible buffeting having thankfully ceased, in the silence he was able to think. Hand still gripping the 'D' ring, he pulled; there was a slight delay before the parachute deployed and then he was really was floating, gently to earth beneath the life-saving silk umbrella.

At 4,000 feet Wing Commander Bader floated through a layer of cloud, emerging to see the ground still far below. Alarmed by the roar of an aero-engine, he saw an Me 109 fly directly towards him, but the bullets he must have half expected never came as the enemy fighter flashed by just 50 yards away. It may surprise many people to know that such a parachute descent, made due to enemy action or some other mishap whilst flying actively, was the first a pilot would actually make, there being no formal parachute training. Consequently, Bader had never before had to consider the practicalities of landing with artificial legs, or indeed one such leg, as he drifted earthwards. Having

had some minutes to ponder this matter, suddenly French soil rushed up to meet him and he hit the ground hard (possibly in an orchard near Blaringhem, to the south east of St Omer). For Wing Commander Douglas Bader, the air war was over, his personal period of operational service having lasted just 18 months. By that time he had personally claimed the destruction of 20 enemy aircraft destroyed, shared in the destruction of four more, probably destroyed six more, and shared in the destruction of another, and damaged 11.

Johnnie Johnson recalled the scene back at Westhampnett: -

Group Captain Woodhall was waiting for me on the airfield, and when Dundas, West, Hepple and the others came back the consensus of opinion was that, such was the confusion and number of aircraft involved, the Wing Commander had either been shot down or involved in a collision.

As the clock ticked on, it became clear from fuel considerations that the two Spitfires reported missing during the radio chatter over France were not going to return to Westhampnett. Reasoning that if flying damaged machines the pilots might land at one of the coastal airfields, Tangmere control telephoned each in turn, receiving negative responses from all.

Douglas Roberts was a Radio Telephone (Direction Finding) Operator at the Tangmere 'Fixer' station, which was, perhaps oddly, located on West Malling airfield in Kent: -

It was there that on August 9th, 1941, we were told that Wing Commander Bader was missing and so listened out for several hours. Our system was basic when compared to modern equipment today, but nevertheless very efficient. The aerial system was a double dipole which, when rotated, would indicate either a true bearing or a reciprocal. Despite our diligence, nothing was heard from 'Dogsbody'.

Flight Lieutenant Casson had also failed to return, but had either of the two missing pilots reached mid-Channel, then there was an excellent chance that they would be picked up by air-sea rescue. If their dinghies drifted them closer to the French coast then it was more likely that the Germans would get to them first, unless their positions could be discovered and a protective aerial umbrella established. Consequently Dundas, Johnson, Hepple and West were soon flying back over the Channel, searching. At Le Touquet, Dundas led the section north, parallel to the coast and towards Cap Griz-Nez. Avoiding flak from various enemy vessels, especially near the port of Calais, a steep turn at zero feet returned the Spitfires to Le Touquet. At one point Hepple broke away to machine-gun a surfacing submarine, but otherwise the only item to report was an empty dinghy sighted by Sergeant West. To 'Johnnie' Johnson, that empty, life-saving, rubber boat was somehow symbolic of their fruitless search. With petrol almost exhausted, the section landed at Hawkinge. No news had yet been received of either missing pilot. Immediately the aircraft were refuelled, the 616 Squadron pilots took off, intending to head back across the Channel to France. Shortly after take-off, however, Group Captain Woodhall cancelled the sortie, fearing that a second trip was too risky as the enemy might now be waiting. Swinging round to the west, Dundas led the Spitfires back to Westhampnett.

For Hugh Dundas, the thought of Bader dead was 'utterly shattering'. He drove back to Shopwyke House 'alone and dejected.'

With no news other than the fact that her husband had apparently vanished, Group Captain Woodhall had the unenviable duty of driving over to the Bay House and informing Mrs Thelma Bader. John

Hunt, a young Intelligence Officer, was already there, having arrived to give some support only to discover that Thelma had yet to receive the bad news, which 'Woody' tempered by stating that Douglas Bader was 'indestructible and probably a prisoner'. Later, Hugh Dundas arrived and with Jill, her sister, persuaded Thelma to take some sherry, which she only brought up again. As Dundas drove back to Shopwyke House he cried. Back at the mess, he and Johnnie Johnson shared a bottle of brandy, but desolation had overtaken the Tangmere Wing's inner sanctum. Across the Channel, there was jubilation.

Amongst the successful German pilots on this particular day, was JG 26's *Kommodore*, *Oberstleutnant* Adolf Galland. *Oberleutnant* 'Pips' Priller, *Staffelkapitän* of 1/JG 26, arrived at Galland's airfield at Audembert to tell him about the captured legless *'Adler'*, urging Galland 'you *must* come and meet him'. Whilst in hospital, at the *Clinique Sterin* in St Omer, Bader was actually visited several times by two JG 26 pilots; he shared a bottle of champagne with them in the doctor's room and concluded that they were 'types' whom he would have liked in the Tangmere Wing.

Previous accounts have stated that the Germans recovered Bader's missing leg from his Spitfire's crash site, but in fact French eyewitnesses confirm that the artificial limb in question fluttered down on its own and landed close to Wing Commander Bader's parachute. The villagers handed the article in to the German authorities, after which time Galland's engineers made running repairs on the leg to afford the Wing Commander some mobility. A few days later, Galland sent his *Horsch* staff car to fetch Bader for a visit to the *Geschwaderstabschwarm* (Group Staff Flight).

Whilst visiting JG 26, Wing Commander Bader was interested to know what had happened when he was brought down. His explanation was a collision with an Me 109, although he had not actually seen the aeroplane with which he had supposedly collided. Galland was puzzled as none of his aircraft had been involved in such a collision. One 109 pilot had been killed, however, *Unteroffizier* Alfred Schlager who crashed at Aire, some 10 miles south-east of St Omer. The Germans therefore conceded it possible that Bader may have collided with Schlager who had not survived to make any report. More likely, however, so far as Galland was concerned, was that Wing Commander Bader had been shot down by one of two pilots, either *Oberfeldwebel* Walter Meyer or *Leutnant* Kosse. According to Galland, for Bader it was an 'intolerable idea' that his master in the air was an NCO pilot'. Tactfully, therefore, a 'fair-haired, good looking flying officer' was selected from the victorious German pilots (presumably Kosse) and introduced to Bader as his champion. However, the German pilots' victory reports were inconclusive, as Galland later wrote that 'it was never confirmed who shot him (Bader) down'.

Amongst the officers present at the Audembert reception was *Hauptmann* Gerhard Schöpfel, who recalls that: -

My meeting with Wing Commander Bader was memorable and one which I well recall. Our *Oberst* Joachim-Friedrich Huth had lost a leg in the First World War, and when the report about Bader being shot down reached him he was sure that spare artificial legs existed in England. There followed a number of telephone calls, during which Bader's capture was reported to the Red Cross, and it was decided that an RAF aircraft should be offered free passage to deliver the spare legs to our airfield at an appointed time and date. So far as I know, this was initially confirmed by England.

When the Red Cross announced that Wing Commander Bader was a prisoner on August 14th, 1941, there was absolute euphoria within Fighter Command, and in particular, of course, at Tangmere where Group Captain Woodhall broadcast the news over the station tannoy. When Thelma Bader received a telephone call from 'Woody', Hugh Dundas, Johnnie Johnson and Denis Crowley-Milling were also at the Bay House. Mrs Bader said simply, 'DB's a prisoner'. Rousing cheers were the heart-felt response.

When the signal was received from Germany offering free passage for an RAF aircraft to deliver Wing Commander Bader's spare legs, Group Captain Woodhall responded so enthusiastically that he even offered to fly a Lysander communications aircraft to Audembert himself. The Air Ministry, however, rejected the proposal out of hand on the grounds that RAF aircraft did not require 'safe passage' to fly over enemy territory.

Gerhard Schöpfel continues: -

On the appointed time and date for an RAF aircraft to arrive with the legs, I was at the *Geschwader-gefechtsstand* in Audembert, having flown in from my base at Liegescourt, home of my III/JG 26. Soon after our meeting, Bader wanted to inspect one of our Me 109s. Galland invited him to climb into a *Geschwader-maschine* and Bader commented that he would like to fly it, but of course this could not be allowed.

Many photographs were taken by the Germans of this visit, which many non-flying JG 26 would later name as the most memorable incident of their entire war. Amongst the snapshots is a photograph of Wing Commander Bader sitting in the cockpit of an Me 109, a German officer standing on the wing adjacent. In 'Reach for the Sky' and other books the object in this officer's left hand has been described as a 'pistol' - other photographs from the same series show that in fact *Oberst* Huth is holding his gloves!

Gerhard Schöpfel: -

When told of our arrangement via the Red Cross regarding his spare legs, he was not surprised when no plane arrived as he felt that high authority in England would take time to sanction such things. He hoped, however, that his own Wing would find a way.

One or two days later, our radar announced a Beehive approaching. The Blenheims flew over St Omer where they dropped a few bombs on our I *Gruppe*. Also dropped, however, was a crate containing Bader's legs which was attached to a parachute.

On August 19th, 1941, the 'Leg Operation' took place when, during a Circus to Longuenesse, an 82 Squadron Blenheim dropped the spare legs by parachute. The Tangmere Wing flew close cover, as Flight Lieutenant Ron Rayner recalled: -

I flew with 41 Squadron on that particular sortie and I remember it distinctly. The legs were dropped over St Omer, and not without ceremony, it being announced over the R/T that Wing Commander Bader's legs had been delivered. We were weaving around the Blenheims and we were acting as individual aircraft, not a cohesive formation as was usual. Then we continued on to the target before turning round for home.

Woodhall signalled the Germans and so consequently the crate in question was recovered and the legs duly presented to Bader. Galland, however, was most upset that the British had responded so

unchivalrously. To his mind, 'bombs and charity did not go together'.

On August 17th, 1941, whilst Wing Commander Bader still occupied *Chambre 21* in the *Clinique Sterin,* a local French girl who worked at the hospital in an auxiliary capacity, Lucille Debacker, handed him a note. The content was astonishing: a Frenchman was to wait outside the hospital every night from midnight until 2 a.m., poised to guide *'Le Colonel'* to a local 'safe' house. Incredibly the note was even signed, by a Frenchwoman, Mme. Hiècque, in her own name. The Hiècques were a working-class French family who lived at the *Quai du Haut-Pont* in a long row of terraced houses overlooking the St Omer canal. Gilbert Petit, a young friend of the Hiècque family, was employed at the town's railway station. Each night he waited patiently in the shadows of an alleyway across the road from the hospital, risking being caught out after curfew. Within, though, Bader had received bad news: he was imminently to be taken to Germany.

Having been given his new legs, on the night of August 20th, he knotted bed sheets together, lowered the makeshift rope out of a window at the rear of the building and climbed down. Squeezing through a small gap between the chained gate, Bader met Petit and together they made their way through the cobbled streets, darkness their cloak. Having avoided at least one German patrol, the fugitives eventually reached the sanctuary of the Hiècque household, Bader in great pain from his stumps. *'Le Colonel'* was given a bed upstairs, before drifting off into sleep he thought 'That's foxed the bloody Huns. I'll be seeing Thelma in a couple of days!'

The following day, Mme. Hiècque walked to the hospital and saw many German soldiers searching for the escaped prisoner. Upon her return, she told Bader that *'Les Boches sont tres stupides!'* Bader, however, appreciated the consequences for these French patriots if he was found in their house. Mme. Hiècque was supremely confident, however, that the Germans would never find him, and awaited word from Gilbert that the Underground had been contacted and an escape plan formulated. That afternoon, *'Le Colonel'* was taken out into the back garden and watched a tangled mass of contrails overhead as yet another drama took place above St Omer. The Hiècques and their neighbours shouted enthusiastically, *'Vive les Tommies! Vive les Tommies!',* giving Bader another view of the sweeps he had flown so often.

The Hiecque's canalside house was actually some distance from the *Clinique Sterin,* and the Germans, being convinced that Bader could not walk far, had cordoned off the area of St Omer around the hospital which they now searched intently. The hospital staff were all questioned, but one female lacked Lucille Debacker's courage and resolve: Hélène Lefevre betrayed the conspirators. At about 5.30 p.m. came an urgent bang at the Hiècque's door - *'Les Boches!'* M. Hiècque bundled Bader into the back garden, hiding him in a chicken run. Within a minute the Germans were in the house and seconds later a bayonet was thrust repeatedly into the straw covering the escapee. Realising that the next stab would probably penetrate his neck or back, Wing Commander Bader stood up, raising his hands. As the Germans escorted him out of the front door to a waiting car, he tried to persuade the *Stabsfeldwebel* (Staff Sergeant) who had arrested him that the old couple had no knowledge of his presence, his arrival having been during the night and via a back garden gate. It was then that he noticed Hélène Lefevre leave the German vehicle, and realised that they had all been betrayed.

Bader's escape attempt made life 'very unpleasant' for *Oberstleutnant* Galland. There was an inquiry

into the escape and even Bader's visit to Audembert, for which Galland had not requested permission, came under scrutiny. For the Germans, however, this was a taste of just how unmanageable and implacable Wing Commander Bader was going to be in captivity, even as a disarmed prisoner.

Gerhard Schöpfel: -

After Wing Commander Bader received his new legs, we heard that he had escaped by knotting some bed sheets together and climbing out of an upstairs window. For a man with two artificial legs this must have taken incredible guts and will power. Really, however, in view of the strenuous activity involved, which included hiking over the Pyrenees, he actually had little chance of getting away with it. He was soon found in a house by the canal in St Omer. Our *Geschwader* was told that on a subsequent train journey into captivity proper, the guards took both his legs away to prevent another audacious escape attempt!

On August 9th, 1941, 616 Squadron's diarist recorded in the Operations Record Book (ORB) that:

This was a very sad day because we lost our much admired Wing Leader, Wing Commander Bader, and Flight Lieutenant LH Casson, 'B' Flight commander and one of the "Originals" of the squadron. Both these leaders were very popular with everyone and their absence will be keenly felt.

At the end of the month, the ORB concluded that August was: -

A disappointing one from the operational point of view owing to the poor weather conditions. Although 16 offensive sweeps were carried out over France, their effectiveness was in several cases hampered by too much cloud, making it difficult for the squadrons in the Wing to keep together. Wing Commander Bader DSO (& Bar) DFC, and Flight Lieutenant Casson were shot down on August 9th and are now prisoners of war. This was a serious loss to the RAF, the Wing and the Squadron.

Following the loss of its first Wing Leader, the Tangmere Wing itself would never be the same again. It is appropriate, however, to let the last word to go to (the sadly now late) Air Vice-Marshal Johnnie Johnson, Wing Commander Bader's No 4 on August 9th, 1941: -

When Douglas was shot down it really was his own fault. He was tired, ready for a rest. Leigh-Mallory had asked him to come off Ops, as 'Sailor' Malan, leader of the Hill Wing, had already done having recognised in himself the signs of strain. Douglas wouldn't go, of course, and so the AOC agreed to let him stay on until the end of what was called the 'season', the end of September when the weather started failing. Peter Macdonald, our adjutant, a former MP who had served with Douglas in 1940, also recognised the signs of strain and had insisted that Douglas, Thelma and he go off on a week's golfing to St Andrews - they were, in fact, booked to go on August 11th. Douglas was tired and irritable, he couldn't see things quickly enough in the air. On the day in question, when Ken Holden sighted the 109s and Bader was unable to see them, he should have let Ken come down and attack as he had suggested. In not allowing this, he lost us six, maybe even seven seconds, by which time the high 109s were down on us. But of course Douglas was a bit greedy and would not therefore allow this. When I was a Wing Leader later in the war such a situation often arose and it made sense for me, if I couldn't see the enemy, to stay put and cover those who could whilst they attacked. This is what should have happened.

Despite the fact that the first Tangmere Wing Leader was now behind the wire, his spirit continued to boost morale: on Johnnie's Spitfire was painted *'Bader's Bus Company – Still Running'*.

When considering such a remarkable overall story, it would perhaps surprise no-one that when Wing Commander Bader was hiding in St Omer, so too was his friend Flight Lieutenant Denis Crowley-

Milling DFC of 610 Squadron. 'Crow' had been shot down over France on August 21st, 1941, and was one of 18 Spitfire pilots lost that day. Taken in by the Resistance, Air Marshal Sir Denis Crowley-Milling recalled that: -

It was in St Omer that I heard about the plan to break Bader out of the hospital. The idea was that England would then be contacted and a Lysander requested. When I heard about it I asked to stay and help. Of course the scheme became impossible when Douglas, who was unaware of this plan, escaped by other means but was unfortunately recaptured. It was a pity as the Resistance's plan could have worked.

Flight Lieutenant Crowley-Milling was more fortunate than his Wing Leader, however, as he managed to make a 'Home Run'. In this adventure, 'Crow' was guided down the 'Line' by the infamous Harry Cole, a pre-war Cockney confidence trickster who became a turncoat, and was later dubbed the worst traitor of the war.

Although Bader's escape attempt was unsuccessful, it was also remarkable for it had been orchestrated not by an organised Resistance group but by ordinary citizens of St Omer. The Hiècques and Lucille Debacker were arrested and interrogated by the Gestapo at the town's *Kommandanteur*. Remanded in custody, all were inevitably found guilty at a military tribunal on September 9th, 1941, and sentenced to death. However, local feeling ran high and after many pleas for leniency, including one from none other than Marshal Petain, leader of *Vichy* France, the Germans commuted the sentences to 15 years for Debacker, and 10 each for Leon and Maria Hiècque. Thereafter, Leon was detained at Diez Lahn prison, the two females being incarcerated at the Fortress d'Anrath. Remarkably, all were to survive the experience and were released in 1945, fortunate indeed not to have either been shot in 1941 or sent to a death camp. The Germans never discovered the involvement of Gilbert Petit, however, who continued working at the St Omer railway station as though nothing had happened.

Having also been captured on August 9th, 1941, Flight Lieutenant 'Buck' Casson was brought before a German General and then spent his first night as a prisoner of war in a room guarded by two German soldiers. The following day his guards drove him to Lille, from where he was conveyed by rail, via Cologne, to the *Dulag Luft* interrogation centre at Oberusal, near Frankfurt. Buck's third night in captivity was spent in the 'Cooler' whilst his clothes were thoroughly searched. On August 21st, he was joined by Douglas Bader, 'but not for long', the Wing Commander being moved swiftly to *Oflag VIB* at Lübeck. 'Buck' himself arrived at *Oflag XC*, also at Lübeck, on August 24th. There, on September 16th, 1941, 'Buck' received news that he had been awarded a most well deserved DFC. His period of captivity was to end on May 2nd, 1945.

Wing Commander Bader remained at *Oflag VIB* until October 1941, when the whole ensemble moved to a new camp at Warburg, near Cassel. In captivity Bader became totally unappeasable, almost obsessed with the prospect of escape. If a legless man could escape, he thought, then it would mock the Germans in the eyes of the entire world. Whilst certain other prisoners were to resent Bader's almost constant 'Goon Baiting', it should perhaps be remembered that whilst able-bodied prisoners were able to let off steam by playing sport or at least walking endlessly around the wire, the legless Douglas Bader could only be a spectator. 'Goon Baiting' and plotting to escape aside, there was no other outlet for his intense spirit. Not surprisingly, he was unable to contemplate merely sitting out the war in the hope of an Allied victory. Douglas Bader wanted to be back up there, fighting.

Whilst at Warburg, Wing Commander Bader was notified that he had been awarded a Bar to his DFC, which made him only the third man ever to win Bars to both the DSO and DFC. At least his very great efforts were undoubtedly recognised.

Stalag Luft III at Sagan, between Berlin and Breslau, became Bader's next camp. There he was reunited with old comrades, namely Harry Day, from Cranwell days, and Wing Commander Bob Stanford-Tuck DSO DFC, the North Weald Wing Leader who had been captured on January 28th, 1942. David Lubbock was a fellow prisoner: -

Douglas would stomp around the camp, then pretend to fall over and have to fix his legs. The thing was that we were digging a tunnel and filled his tin legs up with displaced soil! When he fell, Douglas would take his legs off and in so doing scattered the soil around him. Those legs also came in handy when we were caught trying to get through the wire. In a rage a German guard smashed the butt of his rifle down on the foot nearest to him. It happened to belong to Douglas, and I will never forget the look on that guard's face when Douglas just burst out laughing!

The late Wing Commander Roger Boulding, a 74 Squadron Spitfire pilot shot down over France and captured on June 17th, 1941, relates another Bader morale booster occurring at Sagan: -

It was snowing hard, and we were playing snowballs. Wing Commander Bader was enthusiastically joining in the fun. A young German *Leutnant* then came rushing over with a note from the *Kommandant* for the "*Ving* Commander". Bader, quick as a flash, said "Be a good chap and just hold that for me will you?", holding out his snowball for the German. Instinctively the young officer took the snowball, and then, not knowing what to do and realising that he had made a complete fool of himself, just stood there holding it whilst several hundred prisoners had hysterics! It was little things like that that made you realise what kind of a man Douglas Bader really was.

Inevitably, however, Bader's behaviour became too much for the *Kommandant* to bear, and so this most difficult of prisoners was moved to yet another camp, *Stalag VIIIB* at Lamsdorf, although even this was not without incident. In true stubborn fashion, Bader refused to go, creating a flashpoint situation with the *Kommandant*; as Wing Commander Stanford-Tuck remembered, the 'Bader Factor' came into play: -

He staged a sort of sit-in in the centre of the camp, removing his legs to make it more difficult for them to move him. The guards were by then shaking with rage as they pointed their guns at him. I was certainly frightened for his life. Anyway, Douglas got the message and decided that he must leave. They had an escort laid on, and, unbelievably, he went down the ranks telling them what was wrong with their dress! I'll never forget hearing someone gasp in astonishment: "Good Lord, he's actually *inspecting* the buggers!"

Such incidents represented real flashes of inspiration and boosted morale enormously. All of this reflected a leader possessed of genius. The press back home continued to make reference to Douglas, even though he was in captivity. His story inspired another young pilot who had lost both legs in a flying accident to persevere. So it was that Flying Officer Colin 'Hoppy' Hodgkinson also flew Spitfires in action over France until he too, by coincidence, was eventually captured near St Omer.

Wing Commander Bader's new camp, *Stalag VIIIB* was huge, containing 20,000 Allied prisoners. Peter Fox was amongst them: -

Douglas Bader and I were frequently in adjacent cells in what the Germans called 'Protective Custody', but known to us as the 'Cooler'. We devised a way of passing cigarettes to each other, but on one occasion, as I passed some through the hatch to Douglas, the cigarettes were accepted but a German voice said "Danke"!

After even more trouble, the Germans sent Douglas Bader to the notorious *Offizierlager IVC* at Colditz. There he was reunited with Geoffrey Stephenson, his friend from Cranwell days. Lord Charles Linlithgow was a Captain in the Scots Guards, also imprisoned at Colditz; he remembered that: -

Douglas, disguised as a civilian laundry worker, intended leaving with the weekly laundry truck. But by now the guards were so paranoid about Douglas that they actually lined up the laundry workers and went along the line tapping their legs with a stick. A hollow 'clonk' revealed Douglas!

Colonel Philip Pardoe: -

Having convinced the commandant that he had difficulty taking exercise in the Coldtiz yard, because it was cobbled, permission was granted for Douglas to walk to the nearby village and back, accompanied by a guard. On these walks he would bribe the guard to look away whilst he swapped our Red Cross cigarette rations for corn, which Douglas then stuffed into his hollow legs, and brought back to Coldtiz. There we used it to make very welcome bread.

Captivity ended at last on April 14th, 1945.

Upon liberation, amongst Douglas Bader's first thoughts was the possibility of getting hold of a Spitfire, just to get a couple more trips in before it was all over, or even getting command of another Wing, perhaps one in the Far East where the fighting was still bitterly ongoing.

A telephone to Air Commodore 'Tubby' Mermagen at Rheims, his old Cranwell chum and former 222 Squadron CO, indicated that Douglas Bader was only going one place: home! From Mermagen, however, he learned that the Hiècques and Lucille Debacker had survived their ordeal; soon they would be reunited with *'Le Colonel'* when he flew to St Omer and expressed his gratitude.

For Wing Commander Douglas Bader DSO* DFC*, the war was over.

After a period of leave in England, Douglas was promoted to Group Captain and returned to Tangmere, not to lead a Wing of Spitfires but to command the Fighter Leaders School. He found his old wartime station much changed, and the posting was not a happy one. Shortly afterwards he was posted to command RAF North Weald, and it was from there that he led the famous first peacetime Battle of Britain anniversary flypast over London. Flying in his wake that day were other veterans of summer 1940, including, of course, the 'inner sanctum': Dundas, Johnson and Crowley-Milling.

Douglas knew that he would not be given an unrestricted medical category in peacetime. This meant that he could never serve overseas, which was a pre-requisite for promotion. As his previous AOC, Leigh-Mallory, had been killed together with his wife in a flying accident (by which time he was the Allied Air Commander), Douglas had lost his guardian angel. Continuing to serve in the RAF would clearly be a frustrating and not altogether fulfilling existence.

Whilst Douglas commanded 242 Squadron, in 1940, his adjutant, Flight Lieutenant Peter MacDonald, was a Tory MP. After the war, MacDonald returned to the House of Commons and urged his former CO to join him there. After giving the prospect serious consideration, he decided against a political career, mainly based upon doubt that this would suit his personal temperament and style.

There was a third option: returning to Shell Oil, the company which, 13 years before, had given him employment as an untrained invalid. For this reason he felt a certain loyalty to the company, and he was offered a position in the Aviation Department. This also meant, of course, that he could keep flying, which was naturally important to him.

On July 21st, 1946, Group Captain Bader retired from the RAF. During his wartime service, in addition to his DSO and Bar, and DFC and Bar, he had also been awarded two French decorations, the *Legion d'Honneur* and the *Croix de Guerre*, and was mentioned in despatches three times. A distinguished record by any standards, but especially remarkable in view of the circumstances.

As planned, after retiring from the RAF, Douglas re-joined Shell Oil. In 1952, he was made Managing Director of the company's Aviation Department, based at St Mirren's Court in the City of London. This appointment reflected considerable success in professional life, which must not be overlooked. Douglas was now responsible for a huge fleet of aircraft. Wherever oil was being drilled, aircraft were needed, providing the opportunity for the MD to fly extensively all over the world in his own company light aircraft.

The war had made Douglas Bader a hero, and he remained newsworthy. In 1954, the compelling account of his early struggle against disability, and the story of his wartime exploits, was published by Paul Brickhill, a former Australian Spitfire pilot. The book concerned, *Reach for the Sky*, was a massive success sold all over the world and in many languages. This elevated Douglas Bader from a national to an international hero.

Not surprisingly the movie industry seized the opportunity to make *Reach for the Sky* into a film of the same name. Kenneth More was chosen to play the leading role: -

I admired Douglas Bader. He was to me a Rudyard Kipling figure; you don't find them any more. I understood him. He was a harder man than I am. To me he represented everything that every Englishman wants to be – courageous, honest, determined – but knows that he hasn't the nerve or capacity to be.

He had got his faults – who hasn't? He suffered fools badly – not gladly. He was difficult, impulsive, strong-headed; he was all these things. But I felt that someone had to give him to the world.

During his research for the part, Kenneth More met Douglas Bader only twice, and at no time did the latter ever visit the set during filming. Ultimately, More's portrayal was brilliant, and the film, directed by Danny Angel, was a global success. More did, therefore, 'give him to the world', and Douglas Bader was now a household name in as many different languages as countries. The great man did not attend the premier, however, at which Prince Phillip was a guest. It was not until years later that he watched the film himself, on television and purely by chance. The verdict: 'Rather good, old boy'.

Global projection of Douglas Bader's moving story even inspired the Kanai Indian Tribe at a reservation near Alberta, Canada. In 1957, at a special ceremony, Chief Jim Shot Both Sides bestowed a great honour on the legless Englishman who was made Chief Douglas Morning Bird. Of all the many honours and decorations received by our hero, this was undoubtedly the most unusual.

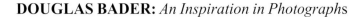

The wartime years, however, were a compelling magnet where Douglas Bader's story were concerned. In 1968, Benjamin Fisz and Harry Saltzman produced the film *Battle of Britain*. Although the film did not portray actual pilots who fought in the real battle but fictitious characters, the producers did engage the services of a number of the Few as consultants. Their role was not only to advise regarding historical accuracy but also help promote the film. Given Group Captain Douglas Bader's reputation, he was naturally invited to participate and did so with enthusiasm.

One problem facing the producers was how to deal with the 'Big Wing Controversy'. Living many miles away in New Zealand, Air Vice-Marshal Sir Keith Park was most anxious about the whole thing, but the 86-year old Lord Dowding was able to visit the set and watch certain pertinent scenes being filmed. On May 26th, 1968, the old man visited Duxford Airfield and there met many of the actors involved. He was also able to rekindle acquaintance with a number of his former pilots, amongst them Douglas Bader. Knowing just how sensitive the 'Big Wing' was, and of Douglas Bader's involvement, all present were concerned regarding how Dowding might react to his presence. Upon the former Commander-in-Chief's arrival, however, Group Captain Bader immediately seized and insisted upon pushing his Lordship's wheelchair, and made it perfectly clear to all they met that the frail invalid was not only the *real* hero of the Battle of Britain, but also his *own* personal hero. As Douglas said to the famous screen actor Robert Shaw (who played Squadron Leader 'Skipper' in the film): -

If it hadn't been for him, old boy, we might be digging salt out of Silesian salt mine. Those bloody Kraut aeroplanes over there with all that language written all over them – that's what your generation would be speaking. At least I wouldn't, I'd probably be dead, but your generation would.

Later in the day, a BBC TV crew interviewed Shaw and Bader. Once the camera had turned on them, for the next few minutes Shaw took no part in the conversation: -

BBC: Douglas Bader, here we are surrounded by German aircraft on an RAF field which must be quite a shock to you. Now there are people who say, after quarter of a century, why make this film, why bring it all up again? What do you feel about it?

DB: Well it's history, old boy, one must show history. If you can show history in a film it's better than in the history books, and it'll be in those things anyway. By all means let's show it in a film, but all I beg of the producers not to do is make it so the Germans win the Battle of Britain, because they didn't. They try to make out that they did now it's all over, but they didn't in fact.

BBC: In a word, Douglas, what's your message as we stand here at this time on your old airfield, surrounded by the Hurricanes that you flew out of here…

DB: Not Hurricanes, Spitfires which I flew out of here, Me 109s which I shot down from out of here….

BBC: And all these 109s round here – what message do you hope that the film and these planes and you can give now, this year, about the Battle of Britain? Everything is sweetness and light between Britain and Germany now. Is it right to bring it up, to remind everybody of the old war and the old animosity?

DB: Well why not? Why not film history? Surely the lesson one learns is that one forgives but that one doesn't forget. It's as simple as that.

BBC: When you were up there in your plane fighting, Douglas, what were you thinking?

DB: Well, I was thinking about what I was going to do when I got back in the evening. That was what I was thinking, old boy.

BBC: Even when you were up in the air?

DB: Yes.

BBC: Was it us and them, or was it your machine against their machines?

According to a witness, the author Leonard Moseley: -

Bader looked at him for a moment as if he was crazy, and we waited for the epithets about the 'Krauts' to come out. But he restrained himself.

The interview continued: -

DB: No, it was the aeroplanes one sort of felt badly about. I loathe those crooked swastikas. What was it Churchill said: 'The crooked cross of Nazi infamy'. That's what one hated. Coming into our skies and dropping bombs on our country and so on. It wasn't personal. You can't hate a chap you can't see, although we all hated the idea of Hitler and the things he did. I mean he was identifiable – but the aeroplanes were just aeroplanes and when you saw them go up in smoke one was delighted and one never thought about anyone being inside them, you know.

BBC: Were you surprised when you found all of these old machines assembled here?

DB: Very surprised to see them here at Duxford, old boy. My old station. They wouldn't have been if the Socialist Government hadn't disbanded RAF Fighter Command. Did you see that picture in the newspapers the other day of these 109s flying over the cliffs of Dover on their way here? I remember thinking that if the government hadn't disbanded Fighter Command a fortnight ago, those K…… those planes wouldn't have flown over the cliffs of Dover, even now. We'd have gone out and we'd have shot the bleeders down.

BBC: Thank you, Douglas Bader.

Leonard Moseley: -

Bader stumped away, waving a hand.
"I can't wait to see the film", he shouted, "It's going to be good. Historical. Only don't let the Krauts win it. We won the Battle of Britain – not them!"
Robert Shaw looked after him for a long moment and then turned away.
"I never knew people *really* talked like that", he said!

Battle of Britain was premiered in 1969, and was responsible for inspiring a whole new wave of interest in the subject. Consequently, in fact, an international cult has since grown around the Few of enthusiasts eager to collect their signatures and meet their heroes in person. Naturally the signature of Douglas Bader remains high on the list of those most collectable.

That same year, Douglas retired from Shell, at which time he was interviewed by the BBC; the reporter had a final question; "Has the loss of your legs been a great handicap to you in your life? Has it prevented you from achieving some ambitions?" The response was spontaneous:-
"Well, if it had, you wouldn't be here talking to me now old boy!"

The company gave him a most generous leaving gift: the Beach 95 Travelair aircraft that he had

often flown on company business. With such a wealth of aviation experience coupled with a mechanical understanding, Douglas was able to establish himself as a consultant. He also contributed articles on aviation subjects to national newspapers, and became a member of the Board of the Civil Aviation Authority.

In retirement, the Baders not only travelled, but Douglas continued playing golf with distinction, his handicap being a remarkable four. Over the years he became in great demand as a golfer, playing with many famous people, including boxers Henry Cooper and Alan Minter, British actors Sean Connery and Eric Sykes, Hollywood screen legend James Stewart, and British & US Open Champion, Tony Jacklin. Douglas also joined the Board of former Battle of Britain pilot and friend Paddy Barthropp's executive car hire company based in Belgravia.

A heavy smoker, throughout this time Thelma Bader was suffering seriously from emphysema. A bad head and chest cold caused sufficient complications to bring the end swiftly. Thelma Bader died on January 24th, 1971. It was the end of a marriage lasting 37 years, one that started with questionable prospects. Thelma's memorial service was held at 'the RAF Church' of St Clement Danes, and was organised by the Baders' great friend and former 242 Squadron pilot, Air Marshal Sir Denis Crowley-Milling. There was a capacity congregation and the papers proclaimed 'The Few salute Thelma Bader'.

No stranger to confronting adversity head-on, golf provided a certain amount of solace and therapy whilst Douglas Bader faced up to his loss. In 1960, Douglas had partnered Joan Murray, now a championship competitor; they made a formidable combination. Joan was also a proficient horsewoman and one of the original volunteers of the Riding for the Disabled charity, of which Douglas was an honorary life vice-president. The pair therefore shared much common ground, and on January 3rd, 1973, they married.

Douglas himself then became increasingly concerned and involved with working tirelessly for the disabled. Three years later, he was knighted for his 'unflagging' work for the disabled. Having heard the news, *Reach for the Sky* star Kenneth More sent a short hand-written note: -

Well done, Old Love, it couldn't have happened to a nicer Bloke!

Kenny

Not content with merely raising money for the disabled, however, as during the war Sir Douglas displayed by example and often raised spirits when at their lowest. An 83-year old Eastender, Nellie Wallpole, was paid a surprise visit by Group Captain Sir Douglas Bader:-

When I lost both of my legs, a friend of mine wrote to you, addressing the letter 'Sir Douglas Bader War Hero – I do not know your address'. The postman delivered it, God bless him. All the letter asked for was a signed photograph of you, but you came round the same day in person! You stayed for tea, leaving me with a photograph of yourself signed 'To Nellie Wallpole, A brave Lady'. When I look at that in the morning I know it's going to be a great day.

In 1981, the courage of a four-year old South African boy, Paul Ellis-Smith, moved Douglas Bader to break his vow not to show his artificial limbs. Persuaded to pose by Lady Bader, Sir Douglas sat

on the veranda of the Ellis-Smith's house in Cape Town, trouser legs rolled up, together with young Paul and another young amputee, student Thys Nortje. Of Paul, Sir Douglas said: -

I went round to their house for morning tea, and there was the little boy, running all over the place, as mobile as anything. In all my meetings with disabled people, I've never seen anyone as mobile as that. I shall never forget the little boy. It was amazing the way he ran about, just as if he was on his own legs. You see, he had never known what it was like to walk on his own limbs, that's the point. It just goes to substantiate what I've always said – if you've got to have some awful catastrophe like that befall you, then the earlier in life it happens the better. It's when it happens later in life that the real problems arise.

The unique photograph was included in another Bader biography, *Flying Colours*, by the late Tory MP and journalist 'Laddie' Lucas, himself an accomplished wartime fighter pilot, who said: -

Douglas is a reserved man in many respects, and does not normally subject himself to photographs with other disabled people, especially showing his legs. But when it came to doing the book, he wanted the picture to go in. He felt that this was an outstanding example of someone overcoming adversity, and that's always been Douglas's line – showing by example. He often recounts the story of Paul to other disabled people.

Indeed, in public Sir Douglas would often refer to 'that remarkable little boy in Cape Town'.

For Paul's parents, Sir Douglas's visit was a moving experience, as his mother, Meg, later said: -

Douglas Bader is a strong and dynamic man… his presence filled the whole room immediately he walked in.

What Meg Ellis-Smith had experienced was the 'Bader Factor', that charisma, enthusiasm and energy that inspired the world. Such humanitarian visits were also in direct contrast to the interview given at Duxford during the making of *Battle of Britain*, which make Douglas Bader tantalisingly enigmatic.

On March 2nd, 1982, a further tribute was paid to Sir Douglas when he appeared on the famous British Thames Television programme, *This is Your Life*. After weeks of careful research and scheming by family and friends to keep the whole thing a closely guarded secret, Eamon Andrews surprised his man at a cocktail party. Sir Douglas had just handed over a cheque for £50,000 raised by the fund raising group 'Sparks', of which he was President, to Action Research for the Crippled Child.

Back at the Royalty Theatre, Sir Douglas was soon meeting family, friends and former comrades, some of whom he had not seen for many years. Although Kenneth Moore himself was prevented from attending due to illness, his wife, Angela Douglas, delivered a message: -

My Dear Douglas

You know very well why I can't be with you this evening. More's the pity! But I'm sending my old lady along to represent me. She's been in love with you for years anyway!

Your inspiration and courage is, quite rightly, a legend. It was with me through the film and is with me still.

"Up the RAF",

Love from us both,
Kenny.

From wartime chums such as Group Captain Hugh 'Cocky' Dundas, the message was clear: -

So long as Douglas was there, morale was always sky high….two words describe Douglas Bader: 'Bloody Marvellous'.

Also present, amongst a guest list including famous sportsmen like Henry Cooper, and even that legendary British movie star Sir John Mills, was General Adolf Galland. After his capture in 1945, Galland was visited in England by Group Captain Bader who gave him a box of cigars and ensured that he was receiving good treatment. As the General said, 'A formidable enemy, but an even better friend'. The General and the Group Captain had met many times since the war, and were indeed good friends.

The greatest tribute, however, came from Clarence House: -

During the dark days of the Second World War, those of you who served in the Allied Air Forces brought hope and confidence to the people of this country through your courage, skill and determination.

In times of peace you have been an inspiration to the young, and have given encouragement and support to many who have suffered physical misfortune.

I send this evening my greetings and warmest good wishes for health and happiness in the years ahead.

Elizabeth R, Queen Mother.

Sadly, there were not to be 'years ahead', but mere months.

On September 4th, 1982, Group Captain Sir Douglas Bader died suddenly and unexpectedly from a heart attack. The man who had been an inspiration and had brought hope to so millions of people all over the world, in a lifetime that defied fiction, was 72-years old.

The Inspiration Lives On

The Douglas Bader Foundation

Not surprisingly, the memory of Sir Douglas's untimely death remains a most painful one, still keenly felt, by his family. For the first time, David Bickers describes what happened on that fateful day, September 4th, 1982:-

Just after lunch, my wife, Wendy, our children (Charley, 17 months, and Tessa, 7 months) and I arrived at the Berkshire farm shared by Douglas, my step father-in-law, and Joan, my mother-in-law. We were to stay the night before going on to a late summer holiday in Cornwall. Douglas and Joan were leaving mid-afternoon to drive up to London where Douglas was to deliver the keynote speech at the birthday party of WW2 RAF Bomber Command's Commander-in-Chief, Air Marshal Sir Arthur 'Bomber' Harris.

As I was taking some things upstairs, Douglas was going up to change. He commented that it was "Bloody early to be putting on black tie and going up to London, old boy, but the party starts at five as it's the old boy's 90th birthday and he has to go to bed early". Douglas always added a 'haw, haw' after something that amused him, and did so.

It was a particularly hot afternoon and I noticed that Douglas was still looking a bit grey. He had suffered a heart attack two weeks earlier at an International Pro - Celebrity Golf tournament. Over supper the previous weekend, Douglas had told us how he had driven into a bunker and whilst pitching out, he had, so far as the people following him were concerned, including Joan, slipped and fallen over. In fact he had actually suffered a heart attack and was unconscious. Afterwards he told us that he heard two voices, one belonging to his friend the golfer Henry Longhurst, who had died a few years earlier, telling him to "Come and join me", and Joan's calling out "Get up Douglas!" Douglas said he told Henry "I'm not ready yet", and got up.

When he died, Douglas' paperwork including all bills was in order and up to date, the bills paid by cheques sent during the week after the golf incident. Firmly I believe, that he knew his time was coming and the 'not being ready yet' referred to his desire to have everything dealt with properly.

Typically on the day in question Douglas was driving up to London and Joan and he would return that night. I say 'typically' because Douglas and Joan attended so many events and functions and very rarely if ever requested a car to collect them. Occasionally for an air show hosted by the RAF Benevolent Fund, a car would be offered and accepted, otherwise they took themselves back and forth.

Just after midnight the phone rang. Wendy got up to answer it and came back into the bedroom stunned, " Douglas is dead". Apparently he had suffered another heart attack, just before the Hogarth roundabout between Hammersmith and Chiswick, as Joan was driving them out of London back to Newbury. This time the outcome was fatal. Joan then had extraordinary presence of mind to go around the roundabout back to the Mews house and had parked in the garage.

Naturally Wendy wanted to go straight up to London to be with her mother and bring her home. This was completely impractical as Tessa was only a few months old and waking up to be fed during the night, so I went instead, leaving Wendy to call back and let Joan know I was on my way.

Arriving at the mews house sometime around 2 a.m., I found two policemen inside with Joan. Within a minute the doorbell went and incredibly I answered it to a man introducing himself as a journalist wanting to confirm a rumour that Douglas was dead! My response was something crass like "No comment", and the chap left.

Joan and I then left immediately for Newbury. On the way down she told me what had happened in the last few hours. She was incredibly composed and strong. They had returned to 'P Mews', as it was affectionately referred to, to change out of evening dress before driving down to the farm. Douglas had said he was tired so Joan was driving. On the way to Hogarth roundabout Douglas complained of a chest pain and died. The first thought after "What do I do?" was followed by an instinctive action, to drive back to the mews. Joan parked the car in the garage and went inside to firstly phone '999' and request an ambulance, and then to phone 'Laddie' Lucas, Douglas' brother in law from his marriage to Thelma, who called the police.

Apparently when the ambulance arrived and Douglas was found to be dead the ambulance men complained that as they were on strike they were only supposed to come out to '999' calls if someone was alive and critically ill! Obviously they didn't know that the deceased had himself contributed to the lives of so many in many, many ways.

Wendy had phoned her sister, Jane, and brother, Michael, both of whom arrived with their families. The farm was the right place for Joan to be. Joan and Douglas had lived there very happily, had their own circle of local friends, and at this sad time of crisis she was now surrounded by her family and her beloved animals.

The journalist who I had spoken to at 'P Mews' had obviously had a tip off via the emergency call or from the hospital, but it was not until 7 a.m. the following morning that the media siege started. The telephone never stopped ringing. The media were very co-operative, however, in giving us, the family, the time that we requested to gather our thoughts and come to terms with what had happened. Later a statement was issued to the press.

The cards, flowers and telegrams, and what they expressed, from friends, people who had met Douglas at some point, even those who had never met him but knew of him, his achievements in overcoming severe disability, his charitable works or his war exploits, were overwhelming, Douglas was truly a public figure and importantly held in great affection and admiration. It was at that point that we all realised we could not let Douglas and what he stood for to us and to so many people simply disappear.

The media coverage over the week-end was full and very moving. Joan was still handling everything incredibly well. The only paper that did hurt us was a Sunday tabloid which showed a photo of a 'Still smoking cigar end and the black tie Bader had torn from his neck as he fought for his breath outside his London mews house'. The 'props' had been placed outside the 'P Mews' house and the photo taken accordingly. It was outrageous.

Both 'Laddie' Lucas and Sir Denis Crowley-Milling were phoning regularly to check up on us. 'Laddie' was the calm voice at the end of the phone advising us on dealing with the funeral and cremation, and Denis caring and protective.

The idea of a charity or fund to continue Douglas' work on behalf of the disabled community formed over that weekend, discussed and debated amongst immediate family .In a sense it gave us all a focus and a goal. Denis drove down to talk it through, although originally I am sure it was to talk us out of it! He felt that the RAF Benevolent Fund should manage a Bader Appeal or Charity. Our view, prompted and supported by the many letters from the general public, led us to want a charity that benefited as many of the disabled community as possible and not simply members of the RAF exclusively. Of course the pride of Douglas' career in the RAF would never be diminished and nor would his post war career and life where he had discovered new challenges and a new happiness as a family man with step children, sons and daughters in law and grand children. Denis quickly came on side and immediately offered support and advice. The Douglas Bader Foundation was formulating (later that year, indicating the high esteem in which the service held Douglas, the RAF Benevolent Fund launched 'The Bader Flying Scholarships' for the disabled, sponsored by King Hussein of Jordan, an initiative continuing to this day).

Eventually we took Joan away with us to Cornwall to get a rest and have time to contemplate and plan.

The funeral was held in Kensington, there then being a very private cremation attended by only family and a few very close friends. Michael, my brother-in-law, and I had a last minute panic and dash late the day before to get the Death Certificate from the doctor and register the death with the Registrar in Chelsea. The doctor told us that "Whilst Douglas was only 70 when he died, he had walked up hill for the majority of his life and his heart was in fact

that of a 90 year old". Certainly we all felt that his death had come too quickly and this did help to explain. Obviously artificial limb technology has since developed lighter and stronger materials as well as limbs designed for various functionality, a long way from the heavy limbs that Douglas and many others were supplied with. Douglas being a double amputee was under particular strain and amazingly had never used a stick or crutches.

The sudden and completely unexpected death of Group Captain Sir Douglas Bader stunned not only his family and friends but also admirers all over the world. Whilst tributes were naturally paid to Bader the warrior, to many it was immediately clear that the world, and the disabled community in particular, had lost a huge and unique inspiration. To countless people Douglas Bader was a vital icon.

Before his death, certain friends had discussed with Douglas the idea of a commemorative statue. His reaction was negative on the grounds that the funds required could be better spent elsewhere. Those now wishing to pay tribute had to take this into account, and it was felt fitting that the 'Douglas Bader Foundation' would provide a living and working memorial to the man who had been, and continued to be, such a huge inspiration to so many. The Foundation's objective became to help and encourage people of all ages without one or more limbs to enjoy as full and successful lifestyles as possible.

David adds that:-

A memorial service was then organised by the RAF at St. Clement Dane's, the 'RAF church' in London's Strand where Douglas' ashes lie, and scheduled for October 27th, 1982. Our aim was to target the service date as the Foundation's launch. This was no mean feat, in fact, as it left only a few weeks. We approached Lord Goodman of Goodman Derrick, who held Douglas' will and acted as his lawyers to become a trustee. Lord Goodman offered to prepare and implement all legal aspects of registering the Charity and for Goodman Derrick to advise us ongoing, free of any charges. He also introduced us to Stoy Heywood who would 'volunteer their accountancy and auditing services for nothing'. For our next trustee we approached Lord Mathews, then of Express Newspapers, a good friend of Douglas' who had persuaded him to write a regular column for The Sunday Express. Lord Mathews accepted and the paper was extremely helpful in supporting the launch.

After much hard work, the Douglas Bader Foundation officially existed, as planned, by the Memorial Service. On that day, our existence, aims and first appeal was duly announced. Coverage was limited as the newspapers were taken up with death of another great person, Richard Burton. However donations certainly came in and each one was replied to with a thank you letter and receipt courtesy of Wendy who had taken on that responsibility. We had approached Lloyds where Douglas banked to open the Foundation account and soon this was growing.

Whilst we had registered our charitable 'object', the use to which raised funds would be put was still being discussed. Wendy and I went to get an opinion from Douglas' personal limb doctor, a wonderful man Dr Merrick Vitali, who had a surgery at Queen Mary's, Roehampton, the centre for amputee treatment and where Douglas himself was treated for many years. Dr Vitali's immediate response was to recommend the provision of a facility where newly traumatic amputees could attend a short - term accommodation and therapy residency environment. Patients would learn from and be inspired by the presence of other amputees and how they dealt with overcoming their disability. Certainly Dr Vitali felt that 'bricks and mortar' were a fitting tribute and he became our Honorary Medical Advisor and another Trustee.

We were recommended to meet with Mr Len Softley of the British Limbless Sports Association [BLESMA]. Len, as we came to know him, was himself an amputee and had been involved with amputee and disabled sports for many years. He certainly agreed with the importance of a residency style facility adding in the thought of a bespoke and permanent site for amputee and disabled sportsmen and women to train. Len also accepted our offer to become a Trustee.

Douglas' close friends from the RAF who had fought with him, by his side in many cases, Air Vice-Marshal JE 'Johnnie' Johnson, Group Captain Hugh 'Cocky' Dundas and Squadron Leader 'Paddy' Barthropp, were asked to be Trustees and accepted. Finally Denis recommended that we also invite Frank Baker, whom he had met through the RAF Benevolent Fund, to be a Trustee and Honorary Treasurer, and 'Duke' Hussey who was then in charge of the BBC and known to both Denis and Lord Goodman. Wendy and I took the roles of Executive and Secretary to the Trustees respectively, and Joan became Chairman of the Trustees.

We still had one further ambition and on February 11th, 1983, Joan announced that Her Majesty Queen Elizabeth the Queen Mother had graciously granted the request to become Patron of the Foundation. A year later Her Majesty kindly accepted an invitation from the Trustees to lunch at the Ritz Hotel giving us the opportunity to personally recognise Her Majesty's support and Patronage.

At our first Trustees meetings the concept of a Sports and Rehabilitation Centre for amputee disabled was discussed, researched and agreed as our major aim, with an amputees visitors network as another goal. It was estimated that £10 million would be required to carry out such a plan. The realities of life were immediately confronted. Competition for public funds was enormous with amongst others, Great Ormond Street were in the throes of their well publicised 'Wishing Well' appeal. Our early experience led us to lower our target figure to £4 million and seek an Appeals Chairman.

Sir Peter Baxendell of Shell became appeals Chairman in 1986, and led a tremendous crusade on our behalf. Separately other fund raising events and activities were held. These included a luncheon at the Guildhall, hosted by the Lord Mayor of London and in the presence of the Duke of Edinburgh, the publishing of a 50th Anniversary of the Battle of Britain book, and our annual Golf Tournament – The Bader Cup. There were also and many others, too numerous to mention in fact but for which we remain immensely grateful.

Justin Cadbury joined the Foundation as a Trustee in 1988, and then, in 1991, we were delighted when HRH Diana Princess of Wales graciously consented to become our Patron.

Finally in 1992 after many site viewings, work on a 'Centre' at last began in the grounds of Queen Mary's Hospital, Roehampton. Raising funds had been a daunting task and we are indebted to Sir Peter for his perseverance. Eventually we saw the rewards of all our efforts and ambitions when on February 25th, 1993, The Dougas Bader Centre was officially opened by our Patron, the Princess of Wales.

With a Centre now in place we needed a Centre Manager and quickly identified Keith Delderfield as our man. Keith had worked for many years at Stoke Mandeville and joined us in a broad role which also involved managing the Foundation on a daily basis. Keith is now our Director of Operations as well as a close family friend.

In 1995, the Richmond Twickenham & Roehampton Healthcare NHS Trust (RTR) accepted financial and operational responsibility for running the Centre. On August 7th that year, the Walking School, a part of the world-famous Roehampton Rehabilitation Centre, relocated to the Douglas Bader Centre. Various other similar groups then moved to the Centre, including those for cardiac, back fitness and stroke patients.

The Centre now provides for vital rehabilitation, the restoration of shattered confidence, and the realisation of how much can be achieved despite the daunting handicap of losing one or more limbs. Facilities assist amputees in the process of coming to terms with their disability, partly through the medium of sport as occupational therapy and also through the example of others, in particular, of course, Douglas Bader himself.

The Foundation's Director of Operations, Keith Delderfield, says that:-

Although Douglas Bader's wartime exploits are compelling and of interest to a great many people, they really just set a benchmark for the grit and determination with which he approached life generally. Perhaps his greatest contribution was when this was applied to helping other amputees, and it is this spirit that now lives on through our Centre at Roehampton.

According to 'Inspiration', the newsletter of the Douglas Bader Foundation:-

Today, the Centre is not only the Foundation's HQ, but it is also a part of the world famous Roehampton Rehabilitation Centre, providing a range of facilities for use by disabled members of the community. These include a multi-purpose sports hall with adjacent shower and changing facilities, a fitness gym, a general purpose area and comfortable licensed lounge. It is well equipped, pleasantly furnished and qualified staff are always on hand to assist individuals or organise group activities. Since the summer of 1995, it has provided a permanent home for the Walking School and a number of rehabilitation and therapy groups organised by the physiotherapy department.

It is difficult to measure the success of the Centre in any way other than by participation. By faithfully applying the Bader philosophy and emulating his single-minded determination, the aims of the Foundation will be achieved and the Douglas Bader Centre will continue to flourish.

By 1995, with the Centre a reality and run by RTR, it could have reasonably been considered that the Foundation had achieved its objective and run its course. Sir Denis Crowley-Milling and several other Trustees, having helped steer the course thus far, quite rightly felt that their roles had been fulfilled and retired from the Board. All were agreed, however, that the Foundation still had new and future goals to achieve and more benefits to offer the physically challenged. In a private meeting, Sir Denis proposed that David Bickers should succeed him as Chairman, and this was formalised at the next Trustees' meeting.

On November 20th, 1996, the Foundation launched the Douglas Bader Grant Scheme, aimed at 'providing support for the pursuance of achievement by those with disabilities'. The Foundation's new Chairman said:-

The Foundation is keen to receive applications from individuals and groups employing similar positive attitudes and philosophies as Douglas in overcoming disability and achieving personal goals. The intention is to establish the Douglas Bader Grant Scheme as a major supporter of the disabled community in the UK.

David adds that:-

We launched 'The Douglas Bader Grant Scheme' to provide assistance, financial or practical, to amputees, thus helping them to achieve (perhaps otherwise unobtainable) goals. Grant recipients are all remarkable people, their challenges varied and many. We are delighted to have helped amputees train for sport, become craftsmen, councillors, undertake challenges that help them and their families, friends and carers overcome their disability.

Appropriately, the event was hosted by Shell International at the Shell Centre, London SE1. There the Foundation's highly respected and much admired President, Lady Bader, was able to present the first round of Douglas Bader Grants.

Amongst those to receive Grants was Nigel Smith, from Aylesford, Kent, who was a right leg above the knee amputee in his mid-thirties. Incredibly, he was a crew member of the yacht *Time & Tide*

competing in the British Telecom Global Challenge Yacht Race. When considering his application, the selection panel was aware of the similarity between the attitudes of Douglas Bader in dealing with disability and the inspiration behind Nigel's decision to participate in such a demanding event. Indeed, it could have been Douglas Bader himself speaking when Nigel said:-

The whole concept of Time & Tide taking part in the race is for the crew to achieve a dream and inspire people all over the world.

A Grant was also given to Steve Johnson from Merseyside, whose intention was to establish a UK five-a-side disabled soccer team to represent the country at international level.

Throughout 1997, there were further Douglas Bader Grants made, and the following year saw the launch of *BADERline*, a new telephone helpline for amputees in the south west of England.

The 1998 round of Douglas Bader Grant Scheme awards included three made in honour of the late Diana, Princess of Wales, The Foundation's former Royal patron. With the full approval and support of the Spencer family, these awards were made to three youngsters, Rhian Jones, aged 14, Mark Hickingbottom, aged 12, and Desmond Brooking, aged 18. All three had demonstrated considerable courage and determination in coming to terms with their disability. Not having allowed this misfortune to hamper progress in pursuance of their chosen objectives would have undoubtedly won support from the Princess, and, of course, this perfectly emulates the example set by Douglas Bader himself.

Today, The Foundation also supports another vitally important initiative for amputee disabled, namely 'CHAMPS'. This project introduces amputee youngsters, aged five and over, throughout the UK to the benefits of physical activity, sport and fitness whilst offering support to their family unit. When considering the prospect of supporting CHAMPS by financing its ambitious development programme over the next three years, the Trustees were mindful of the fact that this particular project would have unquestionably received Sir Douglas' personal and wholehearted support. The great man himself had always been keen to provide disabled youngsters with an early start in coming to terms with and cope with their challenge. He felt that early acceptability of the situation offers the best chance in life and he remained enthusiastic and positive in his encouragement of parents.

Thanks to the financial support received from The Foundation, costs for CHAMPS participants are kept very low. This includes all meals, sports equipment, instruction and good accommodation. It is a commendable policy that the cost of a weekend should never prevents any CHAMPS from attending. The comments of two participating CHAMPS clearly make the whole thing worthwhile to all concerned:-

The best part of my weekend was all of it. It inspired me. I love all sports. It was great to play with other CHAMPS, I can't wait until the next one!

James (aged 12).

I really enjoyed the pool party and I think the whole idea of the CHAMPS weekend is good because it shows young people that they can achieve anything even though they find activities a lot harder than other children. I am very grateful for all the hard work you have put into this weekend to make it possible.

Heather (aged 10).

David Bickers:-

Today I am joined on the Board of Trustees by Justin Cadbury, Sir Nicholas Scott, Stewart Riddick and Christopher Flind. Fundraising continues under the guidance of Keith Delderfield. Our Golf Tournament grows annually and the occurrence of our first Bike Ride in Jordan in 2000 is now going into a second year. Joan is our President and the most energetic President you could wish for, remaining completely committed and pro-active. Joan was deservedly awarded the OBE in the 2000 New Year List for her work for charity, the same reason given for Douglas' knighthood. We are all very proud of her and we know Douglas is too.

In what is a relatively short history, the Foundation has undoubtedly made a considerable impact within the disabled community. Financially, its contribution to date is around £3m. As Keith Delderfield says, however, 'To maintain this level of support requires considerable effort and success in fund raising'. He continues:-

The Charity is fortunate in that it has a number of regular and very successful fund raising events.

Not surprisingly Douglas' long and harmonious association with the game of golf gave rise to the introduction of an annual charity event in support of the Foundation. It is now over 15 years since John Southwick approached Lady Bader with the suggestion of playing an event to raise funds in memory of Douglas. In its early years the event struggled to show an appreciable profit but more recently, thanks largely to Johns untiring efforts as Tournament Director, the 'Bader Cup' has grown to become the leading competition of its kind in the UK and perhaps even Europe.

In the year 2000, the financial contribution of the competition since its inauguration topped the £150, 000 mark. In an attempt to maintain the growth of The Bader Cup, John has made many exciting innovations and attracted support from sponsors, each of whom have played an important part in lifting the profile of the event. The most recent, and possibly the most exciting, has been the introduction of a sponsored overseas final following successful negotiations with the governing body of golf, The Royal & Ancient Golf Club. This proved to be a very significant milestone for the Foundation as it was the first time that an amateur mixed pairs tournament had received sanction to play its final outside of Europe.

In early October, qualifiers from the eleven regional finals played throughout the UK, were transported to The Palmeraie Golf Palace, a magnificent hotel and golf complex in Marrakesh, Morroco, thanks to sponsors, travel agent Marrakesh Express supported by Royal Air Maroc, The Morrocan Tourist Board and the hotel. The final was an unqualified success and it has set the benchmark for future years.

So successful has the Bader Cup Tournament become that a decision was made in 2000 to launch a similar event for ladies only, The Ladies Tunisian Salver. Our President, Lady Bader, a very keen and accomplished ex-golfer, has played a crucial role in getting this competition off of the ground. Thanks to generous sponsorship from Sunnyway Tunisian Holidays the first inaugural final of this new event is to be played at the Flamingo Monistir Golf Club, Tunisia in mid-November.

Each year the popularity of our charity golf event has grown and now, for almost 700 Golf Clubs throughout the UK, it has become a permanent fixture in their annual competition diary. Without the loyal support and interest of the British golfing fraternity the Foundation would find itself in a much poorer situation. Were Douglas with us now he would take enormous encouragement from the fact that such a significant contribution is being made to the work of the charity by a group of sportsmen and women who shared his love of the game of golf.

Last year saw the first of the Bader Bike Challenges in Jordan, which was completed under the Patronage of Queen Noor. Participants, each of whom raised a set minimum of sponsorship, rode over 400kms through the spectacular desert and mountains from Amman to Aqaba in five days.

David Gladwell rode in that first Bader Bike Challenge:-

My dictionary defines 'desert' as, 'a desolate, uncultivated region, uninteresting or barren'. No reference to mud. Sand, I would have expected, but saw little. Endless, unvarying landscape, I would have expected too, but not pure, white, mountains or rock formations of extraordinary beauty.

Why did I do it? I wanted to see whether I could, but I'm sly enough not to let myself in for anything unless I think I have a more than sporting chance of succeeding. I wanted to do something with Olok, which he and I would remember. I'd been lucky enough to see bush, taiga, steppe and jungle, but never a desert. And the idea of working for the experience, rather than just commandeering a jeep, made it potentially the more intense. Moreover, we'd be benefiting a small charity, one that we felt did valuable work: confronting physical disability takes a particular courage and determination.

Jordan is a Muslim country, but in a fairly relaxed sort of way, more like Turkey or 1980s Bosnia than neighbouring Saudi Arabia. The planes of the national airline indicate the direction of Mecca, whilst the stewardesses happily dispense alcohol. There is an Islamic modesty about dress, with which women's lycra cycling shorts are not easily reconciled. You are woken at 4.30 by the hypnotic call of the muezzin, but 20% of the population is actually Christian, and the two communities seem to co-exist quite peaceably. I was told that, 'Jordan is a country of tribes: if you are of the tribe it doesn't matter whether you're Christian or Muslim'. A country of tribes, and to an extent still nomadic. Although the Bedouin are gradually becoming more settled, villages are being built, you still see their goat hair tents, open along one side, singly or in small groups.

On the Monday morning, the forty of us were driven from our hotel in the outskirts of Amman to the nearby town of Az Zarqa, where we were to start our 400km trek. Of Amman we had only a glimpse as we ground through the heavy traffic: a Roman amphitheatre, the appealing mêlée of an Istanbul or an Ankara.

Forty people, aged between 20 and 60, several doctors, three social workers, a hospital consultant, an IT manager, an engineering apprentice, a sports car manufacturer, prosthetists, a limb maker, a photographer, a change-management consultant, three men from the RAF. And, worryingly, all accomplished cyclists; or at least, those who weren't had been training pretty hard. I had to ask someone to explain the gears, and the furthest I'd ever ridden in a day was 30-miles, 30-years ago. However, I reckoned that toiling up the mountains of Snowdonia for eight hours a day was some form of apprenticeship. And if I could cycle in the Blackdowns, the desert would be a doddle. My frail confidence was not entirely misplaced.

Oddly, since our overall direction was to be South, to Aqaba, we spent the first day cycling 80km due East across the desert: first, compacted sand, you just put your head down and galloped, or whatever the cycling equivalent is. Exhilarating. Then, the geological equivalent of *crème brûlée*, a thin layer of lava, broken into a myriad stones. Then, mud. The annual rainfall here is negligible, but, of course, the previous day there had been rain, and it was about to rain again. However, we made it to Qasr al Azraq, the old castle, built originally by the Romans and in 1917 made Lawrence of Arabia's headquarters. Lawrence features large in these parts, if more for his tourist potential than as a hero of the Arab people, which he probably wasn't, except in his own fantasies. The village around Qasr al Azraq has, even in this century, been home successively to Druze from Southern Syria and to Chechens fleeing Russian persecution a hundred years ago.

The second day, Tuesday, was the worst. Up at 5.30 a.m., you'll imagine how I enjoyed that; and it was 3 o'clock before we stopped for lunch, 80km due West on the way back to Amman along the Baghdad Highway. There wasn't much traffic, until recently there was a 300% tax on private cars in Jordan so there aren't many of them, but there were plenty of Iraqi tankers carrying Iraqi oil to the port at Aqaba. 80km of straight, flat road, the horizon always in sight; no villages, nothing to distract your mind from the mounting discomfort of your saddle. The fact that I was 'in the desert' had ceased to be a sufficient novelty: my clearest recollections are of the abrupt edge to the tarmac, and of the yellow reflectors over which you bounced as yet another tanker gusted past. But there were moments of relief. The good-natured encouragement of the lorry drivers, Jordanian or Iraqi who knows, and a couple of 'castles', a term which seems to be fairly flexibly interpreted in these parts. The first, Quseir Amra, was a hunting lodge with rather jolly, obscene frescos (you needed a bit of imagination) dating from the early eighth century: it seemed to be

designed more for hunters of the opposite sex than of fowl or game. It had earned its place in art history, however, because Islam does not allow representation of the human form, hence the development of the wonderfully sophisticated geometric patterns which characterise the decoration of so many mosques. The second, Qasr el-Kharane, conformed more closely to my idea of a true castle, square, impregnable, with handsomely decorated arrow slits; albeit pretty pointless being in the middle of nowhere. But there *was* a point: as Professor Pierre-Louis Gatier comments, 'It was far enough away from the puritanical cities of Mecca and Medina for the pleasures of life to be enjoyed undisturbed'.

The final insult of the morning's cycling was a long steep pull up to our picnic site. Morale was low. As Tom, the young Glaswegian, put it, 'I'm bowdlerised, thighs-wise'. Nonetheless, lunches were fairly reviving affairs: limitless soup, boiled eggs, tomatoes, cucumber, pita bread. The snags were, an obligation to ingest vast quantities of salt (heat exhaustion), processed cheese, a 'mango flavoured' drink (strawberry, if you were really unlucky) and Jordanian tea, ready made with sugar and sage. One serene Bedouin pressed on us coffee, a traditional sign of welcome, flavoured with cardamom: at least the tea was an improvement on that.

25km to go. It's dark by about 5.30. We had turned off the dreaded Baghdad Highway into strikingly beautiful, hilly countryside, bare limestone with some young olive groves; and a village. Jordanians seem to have lots of small children, all knee-height to a cyclist. Mostly, they stared, fascinated by these extraordinary beings: they waved, called 'Hello!' and smiled. But not all. I suppose if one lycra-clad cyclist is quite interesting, by 40 you're becoming bored. Perhaps some of them always carry slings, just in case. One small boy was definitely winding his up as I passed. He hit another guy on the shin: pretty good with a moving target. Gratifyingly, the culprit was scolded by his mother and beaten up by his older brother. In Britain, they'd have been cheering him on.

Unfortunately, this pastoral idyll was too short lived, a long down hill brought us back to the perimeter of the Amman's Queen Alyâ Airport, precisely where we'd arrived on Sunday, and which we now had to skirt to reach our hotel. I realised for the first time exactly how long a runway really is.

Things were definitely looking up. On Wednesday, we were again cycling on roads, but minor ones with villages and reasonable hills. We stopped to investigate the remains of an old settlement at Manjâ, occupied by waves of inhabitants, and with some fine Ottoman ruins still visible. Then on to Madaba, a desert town which essentially grew up around the Church of St George with its remarkable Byzantine mosaic map of the Holy Land. Standing in the shade outside the church, I was approached by an elderly Swedish-American lady, who said she thought that what we were doing was wonderful. Ungraciously, I responded that I thought we were crazy. Her husband had lost his leg in Burma and died eight years ago: his life had not been easy. She had given him Douglas Bader's biography as encouragement.

Our group included five amputees: Chris Moon, who was blown up five years ago clearing mines in Mozambique ('very noisy') losing a hand and a foot, three leg amputees and an arm amputee, a young guy from Yorkshire who coaches a youth football team in his spare time. Of the whole group, Chris was one of the strongest cyclists, and very fit: on our day-off in Aqaba he did a 3-hour run. The only complaint I heard from him was that it would be another 3-years before he could run properly again. His accident was, 'no excuse not to get on with life'.

From Madaba, a climb to Mount Nebo through an archetypically beautiful Biblical landscape (remember those illustrated bibles of childhood?). Mount Nebo is less a real mountain than the edge of the plateau above the Dead Sea, 33% salt and 400m below sea level, the lowest point on Earth. Outside the Franciscan abbey a group of Koreans was singing hymns, exquisitely. Inside, a choir was singing the Battle Hymn of the Republic, badly. On a clear day you can see not only the Dead Sea and the Jordan Valley, the bread basket of Jordan, but Jerusalem and, according to the Bible, the Mediterranean. Moses was shown the lot, in the haze we could only see the valley and the Dead Sea, spectacular enough.

Another long down hill, the daring souls at the front of the field notched up over 50mph, I reckon I hit 15. Lunch with a scorpion, then on to the Dead Sea, oily and impossible to swim in but, happily, impossible to drown in. Just don't get the water in your eyes. The sun sank over the mountains of Israel opposite.

We were accompanied by three guides, a Jordanian, Ishmael, and two Israelis, Gidon, a kibbutznik (played by Anthony Sher's younger brother) and Josse (played by Barry Manilow's grandson). Our mechanic, Ibrahim, was a Palestinian

from Jerusalem. '*This* is the real Middle East', Gidon assured me. They happily talked Hebrew on their mobile phones: I asked if they weren't a little apprehensive. They'd discussed it and decided to go ahead. In the event, no one seemed to notice, or perhaps to care.

I sat at the bar on the beach discussing politics with Josse. He said that Ehud Barak deserved credit for his bravery in acknowledging that the issue of Jerusalem was crucial to the Middle Eastern conundrum. Whether or not these four did represent 'the real Middle East' I have no way of knowing. I hope they do. Gidon was brutal in his judgment of the right-wing Israelis killed the day before by Palestinians at Joseph's Tomb in Nablus: 'It was a calculated act of provocation'. Equally, he was astonished that the Israeli Defence Force should have let them into the area: 'Blame will go very high'.

That evening we abandoned our bikes and took a bus to Petra, police cars fore and aft, 'just in case'. Just in case of what? At seven the next morning we were walking down the long, narrow gorge, the Siq, which until 1831 hid this amazing town from the outside world. Selfishly you regret that Petra is now one of Jordan's major sources of revenue, and three and a half hours is an insult to it. It is hard to recreate the sense of awe which must have been felt by the first outsiders to penetrate its secrecy, you can only stand and wonder at the achievement. Just to see the millennium-old system for keeping separate drinking water and water for livestock is humbling. To absorb the place you need days, not hours.

On a hilltop above Petra we were reunited with our bikes to cross the Dilâgha Desert. But first, Dilâgha, with its abundance of delinquent toddlers and absence of redeeming older brothers. It was all, as Kenny Everett would have said, 'in the best possible taste', but nonetheless scary. The road was steep and, in Australian parlance, 'unsealed'. Add to that, fearless five-year olds playing 'chicken', putting stones across the road, and brandishing lumps of wood at your wheels. However, they seemed to enjoy it.

We then entered a world of white and pink mountains, smooth and other-worldly, one of the most beautiful places I've seen in my life. At the top of a pass, three or four of us stopped for a drink. A Bedouin boy emerged from his family's tent below the road and started talking to Josse. Where was he from? 'I'm a Bedouin.' Which tribe? 'Israeli.' The boy was comprehensively mystified.

Then began the mountain descent, extremely steep, on rough tracks. For those of a nervous disposition like me, it took a long time. Wilder characters, like Olok, fell off, although his only regret was that no-one saw it, or better, photographed it.

As the sun fell, I came to my first real sand, about a kilometre and completely impossible to traverse on a bike. And pushing a bike through sand isn't much fun either. No one was in sight in front or behind. Until, from nowhere, a Bedouin family appeared round a corner, two men, robed and wearing keffiyehs, the younger leading a camel, the older leading a donkey; and some yards behind a woman, wrapped in black. Each smiled politely, as if cyclists were a commonplace in these mountains. It was an extraordinary, touching moment, quite exhilarating. To photograph them would have been crass, but anyway I shall never forget the image.

That night, we camped near 'Roberts' Rock', named after the Scots artist David Roberts (1769-1864) who visited the Holy Land: his paintings included one of this amiable outcrop, then used as a lookout point. After supper, Ishmael created a candle-lit path from the tent to the top of Roberts' Rock, and before turning in, beer cans in hand, we conquered the flickering peak. We slept in a single L-shaped goat hair Bedouin tent, open on its inner side. The focal point was a blazing tree trunk, still burning in the morning. Apart from occasional panic attacks when you awake to find your arms clamped to your sides by your sleeping bag, it was a great night's sleep.

The next day, the fifth, was our last in the saddle, and again over 100km. The first few kilometres were over a rough track, from the Rock to the main road running along the Jordan Valley to Aqaba. If 'valley' conjures up in your mind an image of water, verdure and a gentle downhill slope, so it did in mine. I had, though, wondered idly how the River Jordan flowed from the Dead Sea (400m below sea level, remember) to Aqaba. Silly me. The River Jordan gives up at the Dead Sea, evaporating gently as the easy option. The valley, now the Wâdi Araba, is in fact a rift valley, about 20 miles wide; the only things flowing along it are the Israeli/Jordanian border and parallel trunk roads, one below the

mountains on the Israeli side, the other, 'ours', below the mountains on the Jordanian side, rising to around 4,500 ft. Again, not a great deal of traffic, but when it came, you knew it: 34-wheel phosphate trucks carrying a million tons each month to Aqaba. Fortunately, their keffiyeh-ed Bedouin drivers were more thoughtful than their European counterparts, allowing us a wide berth, waving cheerily. Perhaps because the scenery was more varied than on the Tuesday, the mountains to our left strikingly beautiful, perhaps because our goal was in sight, I enjoyed that last day.

Our arrival in Aqaba, sweeping across red traffic lights under police supervision, was emotional. It must have been. Imagine 40 Brits embracing and kissing one another. Just like Russia. There were even tears. Throughout we had been accompanied by the diminutive and feisty 84-year old Lady Bader: 'Douglas would think you were all bloody mad, but he'd be proud of what you're doing in his name'.

On the last evening, we were admitted to the overbearing Mövenpick hotel, next door to our more modest establishment ('A cosy stay at a comfortable price'; or, 'A comfortable stay at a cosy price', I can't now remember). The reason, an assignation with the Hashemite Royal Family. Queen Noor had been unavoidably detained in New York, 'on a shopping trip', cynics muttered. She was represented by Prince Ra'ad, a Ronnie Barker look-alike. When I was presented to him, he enquired whether I was one of the cyclists. 'Why, don't I look like one?' 'You're wearing a tie.' '*You're* not.' How unlike our own dear Royal Family. Public occasions clearly weren't his forte: I'm sure he'd have been great fun in private. Ishmael had explained to me how the accession of King Abdullah had represented a real improvement in the lot of ordinary Jordanians. Abdullah had never expected to succeed to the throne, and had lived a normal life, much more in touch with his people. He didn't carry King Hussein's weight internationally, but at home he was putting in place long overdue social reforms.

Aqaba, twin to the brash Elat, is a likeable place: the shops are open late, but no one minds whether or not you buy anything, Almost hidden in a few crooked streets is a spice and produce market, vibrant with colour and smells, the traders sitting round chatting. But best of all was the beach at night. On Friday, the Muslim holy day, it was packed with local families sitting around, doing nothing in particular: relaxing. The men played cards or smoked hookahs, children ran around in profusion. Three men passing me asked where I was from, offered me marinated broad beans, invited me to join them.

Saturday was our free day. Olok and I, with several others, took jeeps to Wâdi Rum, described by Lawrence as, 'vast, echoing and godlike'. Granite, basalt and sandstone mountains, weathered into extraordinary shapes, rise abruptly from the sandy desert. Trying to describe the place in words is as futile as trying to capture it in photographs. The drive back to Aqaba, into the setting sun, provided an experience scarcely less memorable, each mountain a sharp silhouette against the next, each more striking in outline, four, five, six deep, from sandstone pink in the foreground through diminishing intensities of grey, charcoal to mist.

The Red Sea is of course not red, but the most intense blue I've ever seen.

We raised £4,630.

So successful was that first Bader Bike Challenge that the second goes ahead in November 2001. Riders must raise a minimum of £2,000 in sponsorship, but what a life expanding and mind broadening experience participation must be. Amongst those riding across the desert this year, I am personally proud to say, will be my wife, Anita.

In a similar vein to the Bike Challenge, The Foundation has been fortunate in securing a number of places for supporters wishing to run the British Memorial 10k Road Race through the heart of London in July 2001. Participants will again be raising a set minimum of sponsorship. Keith Delderfield adds that:-

Those feeling less energetic, but still wishing to support our charity's aim of continuing Douglas Bader's inspirational work of helping the disabled community, or if you think that your business or the company for which you work might

like to pledge corporate support, then donations or covenants can be made in the more traditional way.

David Bickers concludes:-

Nearly 20 years on we remain a charity in Douglas' name continuing to use his inspiration, what he stood for, to campaign and help primarily amputee disabled.

What greater way is there to show continued love and respect for someone?

The fact is that the memory and work of this amazing and truly inspirational Englishman cannot be allowed to fade. Long may the world remember the story of Douglas Bader, and long may The Douglas Bader Foundation continue vital work in his name!

The final word we must, I think, give to Sir Douglas Bader himself:-

A disabled person who fights back is not handicapped – he is inspired!

DOUGLAS BADER

An Inspiration in Photographs

An undated photograph of baby Douglas with his parents, Major Frederick and Jessie Bader.

The Bader brothers, Derick (left) & Douglas, about 1916.

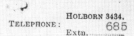

TELEPHONE: HOLBORN 3434.
Extn. 685

Any communications on the
subject of this letter should
be addressed to:—

THE UNDER SECRETARY
OF STATE, Dept. Q.J.

and the following number
quoted:—

A.38255/39/S.7.(e)/2.

AIR MINISTRY, Dept. Q.J.
LONDON, W.C.2

22 November, 1939.

Sir,

      I am commanded by the Air Council to refer to your application for a commission in the General Duties Branch of the Royal Air Force Volunteer Reserve. Your application has received careful consideration and it has been decided to re-employ you, for the duration of hostilities, in the rank of Flying Officer with effect from the date you report for duty and with your original seniority. It is considered, however, that as a retired officer of the Royal Air Force the proper course in your case would be to re-employ you on the Active List of the Royal Air Force and not to appoint you to a commission in the Royal Air Force Volunteer Reserve.

2.   Officers recalled to the Active List owing to the emergency, are eligible, subject to the general provisions of paragraph 3435A and 3546 King's Regulations and Air Council Instructions, to draw the full pay of the rank and branch in which they are re-employed plus 25% of such pay or a rate of pay equivalent to the rate of the retired pay plus 25% which-ever is more favourable. Your service retired pay of £99.10.0 a year will be suspended whilst you are re-employed, but the disability addition of £100 a year under paragraph 3615 King's Regulations and Air Council Instructions will remain in issue.

3.   I am to request that you will be good enough to notify the Department at the earliest possible date that you are willing to accept re-employment under the conditions stated in this letter.

4.   If you are prepared to accept this offer I am to request that you will report for duty forthwith to the Officer Commanding, Central Flying School, Royal Air Force, Upavon, near Marlborough, Wilts, for a refresher course on modern types.

Flying Officer D.R.S.Bader, R.A.F.(Retd.),
    Lensbury Club,
      Broom Road,
        Teddington, Middlesex.

Having graduated from RAF Cranwell, already an accomplished sportsman, Douglas Bader became a gifted aerobatic pilot. In 1931, however, he crashed whilst executing a slow roll at low-level. Consequently he lost both legs, but although he mastered his disability and later passed a flying test, King's Regulations did not provide for disabled service pilots. Unable to accept a ground job, Douglas left the service. As the clouds of war gathered during the 1930s, however, he re-applied for flying duties and, when war was declared in 1939, was accepted. This is the letter confirming his 're-employment'. To say that the effect would be significant would be an understatement.

Flying Officer Bader's first posting was to fly Spitfires with 19 Squadron at Duxford, but he was soon a flight commander with 222 Squadron. Here Flight Lieutenant Bader is pictured (centre) with pilots from his Flight in May 1940. They would soon be in action over the French coast during the air operations in support of the Dunkirk evacuation, Operation DYNAMO.

After Dunkirk, Douglas was promoted to Acting Squadron Leader and given command of the Canadian 242 Squadron. Having suffered during the ill-fated French campaign, morale was low, but, as this photograph shows, the new Commanding Officer (seated with pipe) soon restored high spirits! Amongst his junior pilots at this time was Pilot Officer Denis Crowley-Milling who would become a lifelong and close friend.

The Canadians were a wild bunch; this is Flight Lieutenant Stan Turner DFC, one of Bader's flight commanders. The original caption reads 'A quiet, super type of fellow who never drinks more than he can hold. About three bottles of the finest, third bottle coming up!' Turner survived the war but died in 1985.

During the Battle of Britain, 242 Squadron was a part of 12 Group, defending the industrial Midlands and the north. The brunt of the fighting, however, was borne by 11 Group, covering London and the southeast. The frustration caused by inactivity shows clearly in this photograph of Squadron Leader Bader (third from right) and certain of his pilots. At extreme right is Denis Crowley-Milling (known as 'Crow').

During the Battle of Britain, Bader, supported by his Station Commander, 'Woody' Woodhall, and AOC, AVM Trafford Leigh-Mallory, expounded the 'Big Wing' theory of airborne interception. This involved large numbers of RAF fighters being committed to battle under the leadership of one man, this being contrary to ACM Sir Hugh Dowding's existing System of Air Defence. A bitter controversy ensued, although history has proved Dowding, and not Bader, correct. Nevertheless Wings, each comprising three fighter squadrons, became the standard unit for the 1941 Non-Stop Offensive. A new post was created of 'Wing Commander Flying', and Douglas Bader was amongst this new breed of aerial leader. Here he is pictured whilst leading the Tangmere Wing during the summer of 1941, by which time he had been decorated with the DSO and DFC.

Wing Commander Bader poses in full headgear. The photograph was taken at the 616 Squadron dispersal at Westhampnett, now Goodwood Airfield and Motor Racing Circuit.

Golf was a game that Bader the gifted sportsman was able to play on equal terms with the able bodied, and whilst at Tangmere, on the south coast, he played to relax. Here the Wing Leader drives a ball – hard!

Another Westhampnett snapshot, 'DB' is pictured here between sorties with Squadron Leader 'Billy' Burton DFC, the Commanding Officer of 616 Squadron. A Cranwell graduate and Sword of Honour recipient, Burton was sadly killed in 1943 and remains 'Missing'.

During the summer of 1941, Fighter Command 'reached out', taking the war to the Germans over France. Douglas Bader was at the forefront of developing tactics, and responded enthusiastically to the challenge. Here a 'Finger Four' of Spitfires leaves Westhampnett, presumably for an operational flight.

Each Wing Leader painted their initials on their aircraft to assist with rapid identification in the air. This is Spitfire P7666 *Manxman*, the Wing Leader's callsign becoming 'Dogsbody'.

This aircraft is believed to be Spitfire W3185, *Lord Lloyd 1*, the Mk VA in which 'DB' was brought down over France on August 9th, 1941. Here Wing Commander Bader, wearing black pre-war flying overalls, climbs out of his cockpit after a sortie. The pennant indicates that this is the Wing Leader's fighter.

The stress, however, was bound to tell, and on August 9th, 'DB' made several errors of judgement that led to his Spitfire being brought down over the area of St Omer. Although the circumstances, given the speed of combat, have yet to be satisfactorily explained, the Germans suggested that Oberfeldwebel Walter Mayer might have shot down Wing Commander Bader, pictured here. The Non-Stop Offensive of 1941, was not, in fact, a great success, and that year the RAF lost a number of combat experienced and gifted leaders either killed or captured.

With his tail-less Spitfire spinning uncontrollably, 'DB' not surprisingly experienced great difficulty in safely abandoning his machine. His problems were compounded when one of his artificial legs became stuck in the cockpit, trapping him. With Herculean strength, Bader actually broke the leg's harness and tumbled clear of the doomed Spitfire. After his capture, the Germans were curious to meet the legless Wing Commander, and so repairs were carried out to the leg found in the wreckage of his aircraft. Mobile again, 'DB' visited the German airfield at Audembert, near Calais, where he met *Oberst* Adolf Galland, the *Kommodore* of *Jagdgeschwader* 26. Here the captive Bader is pictured with Galland (the latter at sixth from left) and his officers.

Amongst the German officers present was *Oberst* Joachim-Friedrich Huth (at extreme right), a Great War fighter pilot who was also still flying despite having an artificial leg.

DB checking out one of Galland's Me 109 fighters.

During a bombing raid on the German fighter base at St Omer, a spare pair of legs for Wing Commander Bader was dropped from a Blenheim. Here *Luftwaffe* personnel open the crate, which landed safely by parachute.

Since being captured, DB had been held at the Clinique Sterin, in St Omer. With his new legs, a nurse working in concert with brave local people who were not associated with the formal Resistance movement facilitated Bader's escape. This photograph was taken by the Germans the morning after Wing Commander Bader climbed out of his second story window and escaped!

DB was hidden in this house, 196 Quai du Haut-Pont, St Omer, by Madame Hiècque. Betrayed by another nurse, these brave French patriots were arrested and 'Le Colonel' re-captured.

Back at Tangmere, Wing Commander Bader's presence was sorely missed. Amongst Bader's up and coming fighter pilots was Pilot Officer JE 'Johnnie' Johnson who maintained his idol's spirit within the Wing: *Bader's Bus Co – Still Running*!

Douglas Bader became a real thorn in the Germans' side during the long years of captivity. After repeated but always unsuccessful bids to escape, he found himself incarcerated in the formidable Colditz Castle. There, in April 1945, the advancing Americans freed him. Returning home, Douglas found the RAF much changed, and was unable to settle in any appointment. The highlight of that period, however, was in September 1945, when he led the RAF Spitfire fly past over London, commemorating the Battle of Britain. Here he swings his right leg into Spitfire 'DB' at North Weald for that memorable sortie. For one last time, a Bader 'Big Wing' would soon fly over the capital, and in DB's wake were many friends from the halcyon days: Johnson, Cowley-Milling, Dundas, Turner, Stanford-Tuck and Brothers to name but a few of the Few.

With the war over, the service had lost that purpose that DB found so invigorating. He therefore decided to retire from the RAF, as a Group Captain, in 1946, returning home to his wife, Thelma, whom he married in 1933.

When he left the RAF after his accident, DB found employment with the Asiatic Petroleum Company (Shell). It was to this concern that he now returned, becoming 'Advisor, Group Aircraft Operations'. The job involved travelling extensively around the world, DB personally flying a company Proctor communications aircraft. This Douglas thoroughly enjoyed, and he soon became an unofficial ambassador not only for the UK, but also equally for the disabled community.

DB's Proctor.

DB pictured in 1950. A maturing man of experience and confidence, he n e v e r t h e l e s s resisted all efforts to persuade him to go into politics.

Amongst the various functions attended by DB during his time with Shell was the launching of the 'Hemiglypta', one of the company's general-purpose tankers on October 12th, 1954. This took place at the yard of Messrs. Cammell Laird and Co at Birkenhead. The naming and launching ceremony was performed by Lady White OBE, the wife of His Excellency The Hon Sir Thomas White, High Commissioner for Australia. Here DB is pictured in conversation with His Excellency's wife, Lady White OBE. By this time DB was a household name given the enormous success of the book and film about his life, *Reach for the Sky*.

When DB eventually retired from Shell, the company generously gave him the light aircraft, a Beech Travelair that he had flown around the world on their behalf. He is pictured here with that aircraft, G-APUB.

DB in his element: at the controls of G-APUB.

Understandably the wartime years remained a big pull for DB. In 1964, Group Captain Bader returned to St Omer and visited those brave people who had helped him escape. He is pictured here with Madam Hiècque, who was invested with the *Legion d'Honneur*. DB was made an honorary citizen of the town.

After the war, the large number of war films released and wartime memoirs published stimulated a great interest in those august events. Former fighter 'aces' found themselves in demand all over the world at symposiums, air shows and other events. Here DB is pictured with his old former adversary, General Adolf Galland.

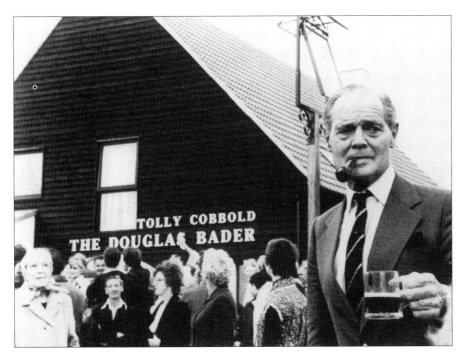

Given his inspirational story and the huge success of *Reach for the Sky*, DB became the fighter pilot icon. People the world over were fascinated and inspired by the story of how this gutsy young man overcame his disability and argued his way back into the cockpit of an RAF fighter. Hundreds of tributes were paid to him, including the naming of a public house situated near Tangmere in Sussex.

DB, who did not drink alcohol, nevertheless pulled the first pint! Pictured at right is his second wife, Joan. Thelma Bader died in January 1971.

In 1968, the film *Battle of Britain* was made. The producers commissioned a number of the Few to not only act as advisors but also promote the film. Amongst them, of course, was DB, pictured here at Duxford with a line up of 'German Me 109s'. According to his great friend (the sadly now late) 'Laddie' Lucas, Douglas himself was particularly proud of this picture in which he appeared completely able-bodied.

Men in black or a gathering of eagles? General Galland, Group Captain Bader, unknown, and Air Vice-Marshal Johnnie Johnson. The latter finished the war as the RAF's official top scoring fighter pilot.

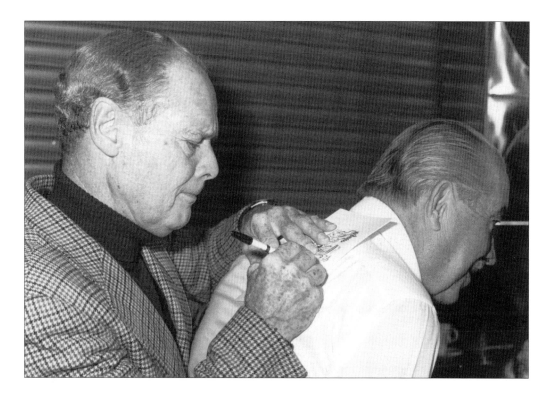

Autographs, always autographs wherever these great men were seen. Here General Galland's back provides an impromptu table for DB.

DB signing a copy of Paul Brickhill's best seller, *Reach for the Sky*.

Joan Bader pictured with her parrot, 'Charlie', whose 'kills' included such fighter 'aces' as Johnnie Johnson and Bob Stanford-Tuck!

Aces: General Galland, Wing Commander Geoffrey Page, DB and Wing Commander Bob Stanford-Tuck. All are now deceased.

The same line up pose with a Spitfire at an air show, clearly re-living old times.

The aces are driven around the crowd line. As always, DB is in the front seat and appears the most enthusiastic!

Johnnie Johnson and DB at an RAF function.

A formal photograph of DB taken for publicity purpose when his own book, *Fight for the Sky*, was released in 1973.

Signing yet another copy of *Reach for the Sky*!

A pensive DB, pen as ever at the ready.

With Joan, unveiling yet another tribute.

DB and Joan at an annual Battle of Britain Fighter Association reunion dinner.

At another Fighter Association event, Her Majesty the Queen Mother is greeted by 'Forces' Favourite' Dame Vera Lynn and DB in 1973.

One of my personal favourites: HM the Queen Mother dancing with DB at RAF Bentley Priory.

Proud moment: Douglas and Joan with HM the Queen Mother, Patron of the Battle of Britain Fighter Association.

MRAF Sir Ivor Broom and DB with HM the Queen Mother.

At yet another function, Douglas and Joan with Wing Commander 'Paddy' Barthropp and his wife, Betty.

DB with the young Prince of Wales.

Still an inspiration to the RAF: DB with RAF Battle of Britain Memorial Flight personnel, probably at RAF Coltishall.

'Now that's how you do it, old boy'. DB shows a would-be fighter pilot into the cockpit of the RAF Museum's Spitfire Mk IA.

In the 'office', DB points out the instruments and controls.

The bronze bust of DB on show at the RAF Museum, Hendon.

DB doing what he did best: inspiring.

Johnnie Johnson (second left) and DB with the singer Ann Shelton. DB would appear to be in good voice!

DB, Johnnie, Adolf Galland and friend enjoying life to the full.

The serious side: DB gets the message across during a visit to the San Antonio Air Force Base, USA.

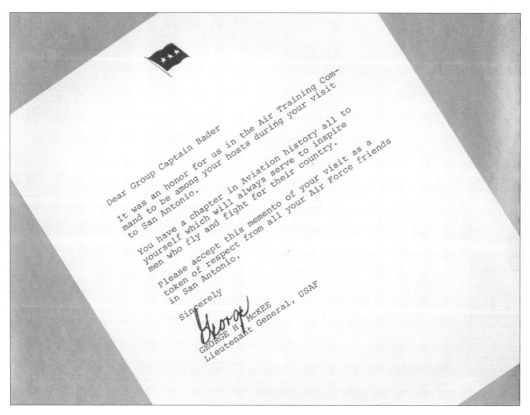

Dear Group Captain Bader

It was an honor for us in the Air Training Command to be among your hosts during your visit to San Antonio.

You have a chapter in Aviation history all to yourself which will always serve to inspire men who fly and fight for their country.

Please accept this memento of your visit as a token of respect from all your Air Force friends in San Antonio.

Sincerely

George

GEORGE H. McKEE
Lieutenant General, USAF

The letter of appreciation received by DB following his San Antonio visit.

With a Confederate Air Force pilot and Mosquito at Randolph Air Force Base, Texas, USA.

DB was made a Colonel of the CAF.

Back home, DB was frequently called upon at Remembrance time to participate in commemorative events.

DB lays a wreath at a USAAF ceremony.

DB leaving Westminster Abbey after an annual service on Battle of Britain Sunday. Behind him is his lifelong friend, Air Marshal Sir Denis Crowley-Milling. The pair fought side-by-side during that fateful summer of 1940.

In complete contrast, DB and Joan in Africa with native tribesmen.

Joan in Red Indian regalia at a local event in Berkshire.

An early photograph of Joan and DB taken on the golf course. This was their first competition together, at Roehampton – they won!

DB and golfing chums.

DB golfing with Henry Cotton (second left) and Victor, the Lord Matthews.

DB with Sir Alec Douglas-Hume, 1980.

With comedian Jimmy Tarbuck (second left) and Michael Medwin. Golf, like all sports, bonds together those with a common interest.

With screen legend Sean Connery at St Andrew's.

DB walking the greens, a daunting prospect on some courses for the able bodied!

Did DB walk or use the buggy, I wonder?

Playing in the Marley Trophy with Lee Trevino, Seve Ballesteros and Bruce Forsyth.

That pensive look again. The perceptive will have noticed by now that DB has several different faces for the camera.

This is perhaps the most revealing face of all!

DB whilst Managing Director of Shell Aircraft Ltd., 1968.

DB throws the Haggis!

A trendy DB complete with pipe and Hush Puppies.

DB was, I am told, an excellent dinner companion.

A talented cricketer himself before his accident, DB enjoys an afternoon of village cricket at Bucklebury.

HRH Princess Alice, Duchess of Gloucester, opens the Douglas Bader Wing, April 1976.

Overseas again, as ever surrounded by the press and happy faces.

Bader the orator.

That pensive look again!

Joan and Douglas pictured at their farmhouse in Berkshire.

At Abbotsford Air Show, August 1977!

Swimming in Australia – without legs.

DB receives an Honorary Degree from the University of Calgarry.

That DB's story inspired people all over the world is evident by these pictures taken during the ceremony in which he became Chief Morning Bird!

DB made friends easily and with people from all races, creeds and cultures: Chief Shot Both Sides.

DB outside the teepee of Chief Shot Both Sides and his wife, Rosie.

DB's first time on horseback, Bluebird Hill, Australia.

Ride 'em cowboy! The Baders on horseback in Canada.

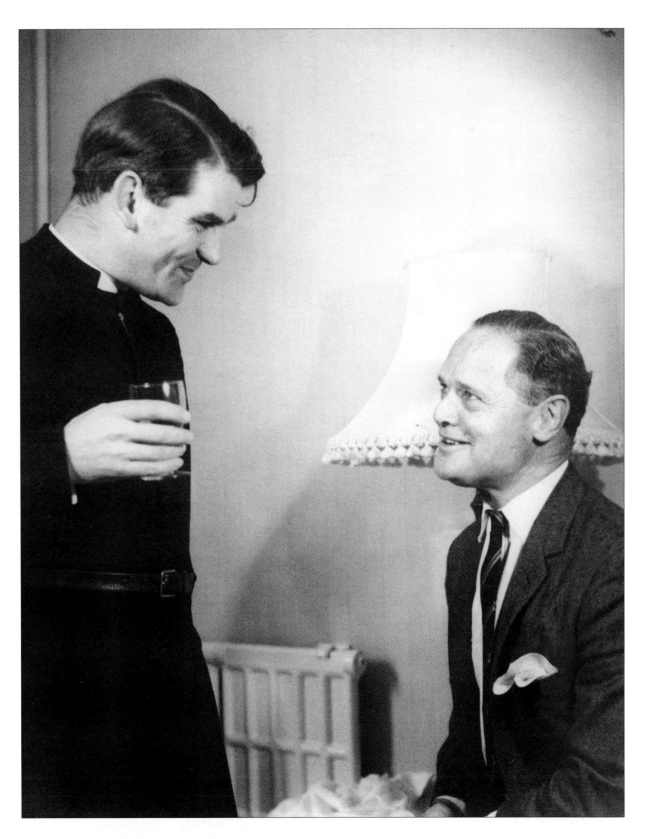

DB's friends even extended to members of the clergy: here he is pictured with The Rev Tom Ekin, now Vicar at Englefield, Berks. DB was Godfather to one of his son's.

With the Lord Mayor of London.

A rare picture indeed – DB in a wheelchair! The occasion was a 100-mile wheelchair push for charity.

The Baders with friends including an obviously inspired young man with a physical challenge.

The only photograph ever taken of DB's artificial limbs: with little Paul Ellis-Smith and Thys Nortje in South Africa, 1981. Both amputees remain inspired by his visit, 20 years on.

Inspiring disabled youngsters at the Regency Park Centre, 1978.

Inspiring disabled children in South Africa. It was for this kind of work – not his wartime or flying exploits – that DB was knighted in 1976.

At the Scholfields Air Show in Australia, 1981.

Back home, DB was a happy family man. He had become stepfather to Joan's two daughters, and poses here, on his 70th birthday (February 21st, 1980), with his first step-grandson. The great man appears both moved and delighted.

On March 2nd, 1982, DB was 'ambushed' at a charity function by *This Is Your Life* TV presenter Eamon Andrews.

Joan and Douglas on set at the start of the programme, filmed at the Royal Theatre, London.

DB greeted by his great friends, Wing Commander PB 'Laddie' Lucas and his wife, Jill (he was related to the latter through marriage to Thelma).

Unfortunately the great British actor Kenneth Moore, who played Douglas in the film *Reach for the Sky*, was too ill to attend, but sent a message of greeting with his wife, Angela Douglas.

With AVM Sir Harry Broadhurst. Once nursing a shrapnel riddled backside, 'Broadie' was not amused when DB chortled that if he stopped running away from the enemy he wouldn't get hit in the a**e!

Greeting Group Captain Hugh 'Cocky' Dundas, another lifelong friend from the Battle of Britain and beyond. Shot down and wounded during the summer of 1940, Dundas later found Bader immensely inspiring whilst coming to terms himself with being back in the air on operations.

With AVM Johnnie Johnson and Sir Alan Smith. With DB, Dundas, Johnson and Smith were the other members of the fabled Tangmere Wing's 'Dogsbody Section'. When young Sergeant Smith was told to be the Wing Leader's No 2, he considered it akin to 'God asking me to look after heaven for him!'

Dogsbody Section with the New Zealander Jeff West, who took Alan Smith's place as No 2 on the sortie during which the Wing Leader was brought down and captured.

With General Adolf Galland. As a result of DB's escape attempt, having previously entertained him at Audembert, Galland found himself in trouble with his *Luftwaffe* masters.

With Air Commodore Al Deere, a most distinguished Battle of Britain 'ace' from New Zealand who fought in 11 Group.

Madame Pettit, widow of Gilbert (who met DB clandestinely, by prior appointment, and helped him through the blacked-out streets of St Omer to Madame Hiècque's safe house).

Chief Shot Both Sides and his wife, Rosie.

Lifelong friend, comrade and colleague, the flamboyant Paddy Barthropp.

With British screen legend Sir John Mills, who received his Knighthood on the same day as Sir Douglas.

'Group Captain Sir Douglas Bader, This Is Your Life'!

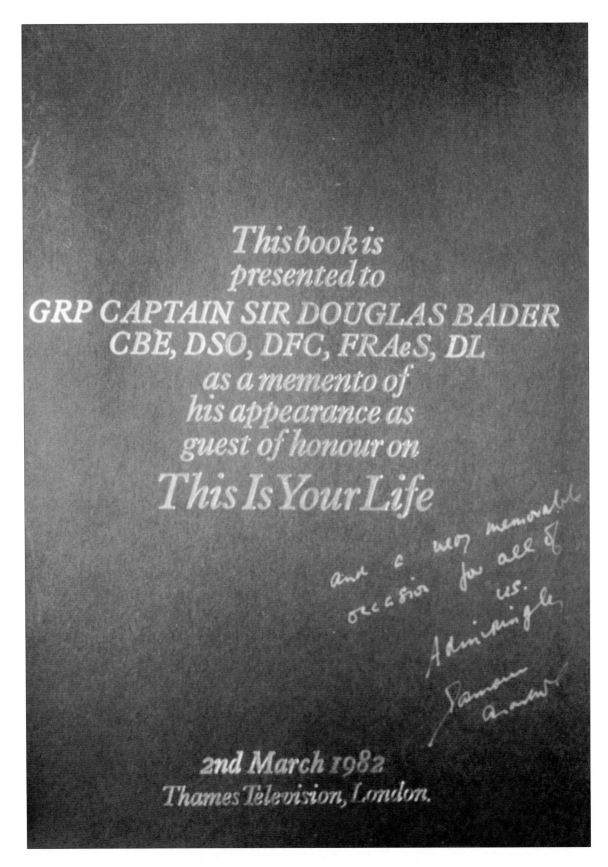

The inscription appearing within that unique 'Red Book'.

The Red Book together with an RAF officer's cap badge once belonging to Sir Douglas himself.

It is a fact that the Few, and Douglas Bader in particular, set the benchmark against which all future military pilots would be judged. On August 31st, 1982, the Baders were guests at RAF Finningly.

Sadly not even Douglas Bader could not go on forever. Having 'walked up hill' for most of his life, Group Captain Sir Douglas Bader died of a heart attack on September 4th, 1982. This picture was taken towards the end of this great life, and shows a man apparently older than his actual 72 years. As the photographs in this book clearly show, this was a man who lived life to the full and in the fast lane. A man who had fought for his country, defying gravity in the process, and had travelled all over the world. An exhausting prospect for an able-bodied person, it should not be forgotten that all of this 'DB' achieved without legs.

Death, however, did not suppress either the inspiration or admiration, and many people wanted to pay tribute to Douglas. On August 11th, 1984, for example, Lady Bader officially opened Bader Close in Stevenage, Herts.

At RAF Coltishall, a station from which DB flew in 1940 and 1941, a replica of his famous 242 Squadron Hawker Hurricane, LE-D, was also unveiled.

At the Bader Arms, Tangmere, the sign was changed because Douglas decreed the picture to be '****** awful'! On that occasion, Lady Bader is joined by Group Captain Hamish Mahaddie (with bowler hat), Air Chief Marshal Sir Christopher Foxley-Norris and Paddy Barthropp.

Although his wartime exploits remain relatively well known, like DB, less recognised is Johnnie Johnson's work for the elderly and infirm. After leaving the RAF, Johnnie founded the Johnnie Johnson Housing Trust, which now manages over 4,000 properties. Here Joan and Johnnie are pictured with the Trust's John Roberts prior to the opening of 'Bader Court', a sheltered housing development in Blyth, Northumberland.

Douglas Bader's family and friends decided to pay their personal tribute by way of founding The Douglas Bader Foundation, a living memorial which would benefit the disabled (and in particular amputee) community. The intention was to create a Douglas Bader Centre for sports and rehabilitation, and uphold DB's story as an inspiration to the disabled. In 1983, appeals were launched towards achieving that far-sighted goal. This photograph was taken at London's Mansion House, and includes the following supporters: Lord Mayor of London (elect), Lady Mayor (elect), AVM JE Johnson, The Lord Goodman, Wing Commander PP Barthropp, The Lady Mayor, The Lord Mayor of London, AM Sir Denis Crowley-Milling, HRH the Duke of Edinburgh, Lady Bader, Group Captain HSL Dundas, Mr DCT Bickers & Dr M Vitali.

The Appeal led to many and varied donations. Here Lady Bader accepts a cheque from the RAF Careers Information Service.

In 1984, The Douglas Bader Foundation was formalised and launched at the RAF Museum, Hendon. Pictured with a young amputee on that happy occasion are, from left, Group Captain Sir Hugh Dundas, Air Marshal Sir Denis Crowley-Milling and Air Vice-Marshal Johnnie Johnson.

The appeal was ultimately successful and sufficient funds were raised to create The Douglas Bader Centre at Queen Mary's Hospital, Roehampton. The Centre was opened by the (tragically now late) HRH Diana, Princess of Wales, in 1993.

DOUGLAS BADER: *An Inspiration in Photographs*

That the Centre has been a success is evident from these photographs of sport in progress.

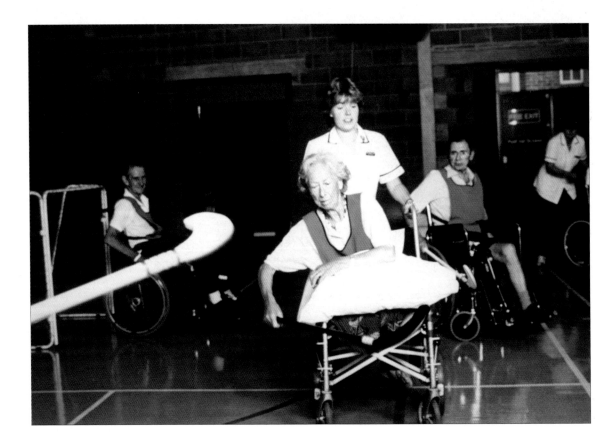

Having achieved the Centre, the Foundation then launched the Douglas Bader Grant Scheme, aimed at helping disabled people achieve their goals, such as Andrew Brown, pictured here (see foreword).

Another Grant Scheme recipient has been Dundee's Tommy McKay, pictured here on a dragline whilst training with the GB Disabled Wintersport/Ski Squad at Tigne in the French Alps.

Grant recipient Nigel Smith was a disabled crewmember on *Time & Tide*, a yacht competing in the British Telecom Global Challenge Yacht Race.

Lady Bader pictured with Nigel on board *Time & Tide* upon completion of the epic voyage.

Lady Bader with some Grant Scheme beneficiaries at the Douglas Bader Centre: Nigel Smith (*Time & Tide* crewmember), Diane Corrick (Education Grant for a counselling qualification), Mark Hickingbottom (watersports), Desmond Brooking (Education Grant, art student), Glen Burridge (Sports Coaching Degree), Rhian Jones (swimming), Len Softley MM, BEM (Trustee DBF).

Not surprisingly given the Baders' love of the game, The Bader Foundation has benefited from fund raising within this sport. The annual Bader Cup has become the leading competition of its type in Europe, and perhaps beyond. Here Lady Bader lines up for her famous drive, thus opening the new course at Ormonde Fields Golf Club.

Lady Bader pictured at Bransford Golf Club, Worcester, at a qualifying round in 2000. With her are, from left, Mohammed Knichich, Managing Director of Marrakech Express (the Bader Cup's main sponsors in both 2000 & 2001), John Southwick, the Bader Cup's Tournament Director, and Keith Delderfield, the Foundation's Director of Operations.

John Southwick has worked tirelessly for the Bader Cup Tournament for many years, and the competition's success is directly attributable, in the main, to his efforts. Here John presents Lady Bader with a cheque for £15,000.

The Bader Bike Challenge is rapidly becoming another popular fund raising initiative. Riders cover some 200 miles through the Jordanian Desert, each having first raised £2,200 in sponsorship. One participant in the first Challenge, which took place in 2000, was the RAF BBMF's Jamie Farr. Pictured here with Lady Bader at RAF Coningsby, the Flight's base, are, from left, Rev Andy McMullen, Jamie Farr, and the Commanding Officer, Squadron Leader Paul Day OBE AFC.

Participants set off on Day One of the Bader Bike Challenge, 2000. At centre, on tandem, is the Foundation's Operations Director Keith Delderfield and his wife, Jess.

153

The 'Jordan 2000 Team' with Lady Bader at Robert's Rock, 6 a.m. on the Challenge's final day – next stop Aqaba, only 85 miles!

Bader Bike Challenge participants must raise a minimum of £2,200 in sponsorship (and many raise much more). Fund raising activities all over the country therefore raise awareness of the Foundation's work, and represents most welcome publicity. Here the author's wife, Anita, is pictured training for the 2001 Bader Bike Challenge with Nicola Fone, her Personal Trainer, at the Abbey Court Fitness Centre. The photograph appears courtesy of the Worcester Evening News and illustrated an article about the Challenge in that newspaper.

The Bader Bike Challenge takes place under the patronage of Queen Noor of Jordan, whose late husband, King Hussein, was a friend and admirer of Douglas Bader's. Queen Noor is pictured here at the Centre, making a Grant Scheme presentation to a grateful recipient. At centre is the Foundation's Chairman, Douglas Bader's step-son-in-law, David Bickers.

As a token of appreciation, David Bickers presents Queen Noor with a framed print of Robert Taylor's 'Bader's Bus Company'.

Another important initiative supported by the Foundation is CHAMPS, a project introducing amputee youngsters, aged five and over, to the benefits of sport and fitness whilst offering support to the family unit. Here CHAMPS enjoy themselves at the Oasis Centre in Swindon.

Fund raising goes on and on, however. All donations are gratefully received, including this cheque from pupils of The Patrick Gibson Guitar School in Tring, Herts, following a concert.

156 DOUGLAS BADER: *An Inspiration in Photographs*

The story of Douglas Bader remains well known amongst aviation enthusiasts and during the 1990s this author did much to maintain, stimulate and extend this interest. Two of his 13 previous books, in fact, concern DB. Generously, Dilip has waived all future Royalty rights in respect of both these previous works and this new book in favour of the Foundation. He is pictured here with Lady Bader at the launch of his eighth book, *Missing in Action: Resting in Peace?* at Worcester Guildhall in 1998. Former wartime pilots pictured are Flight Lieutenants Richard Jones, Gordon Batt, (the late) Ron Rayner, Geoffrey Stevens and Mr Peter Fox.

In 1996, Dilip Sarkar led an operation to locate and recover for conservation the remains of the Spitfire in which Douglas Bader was brought down over France. A site was consequently excavated near St Omer, and the substantial remains of a Spitfire recovered. Unfortunately the aircraft transpired not to be Wing Commander Bader's, but one shot down nearly two years later. Nevertheless, the project was a tremendous experience for all involved and uplifted the Foundation's profile due to the publicity arising.

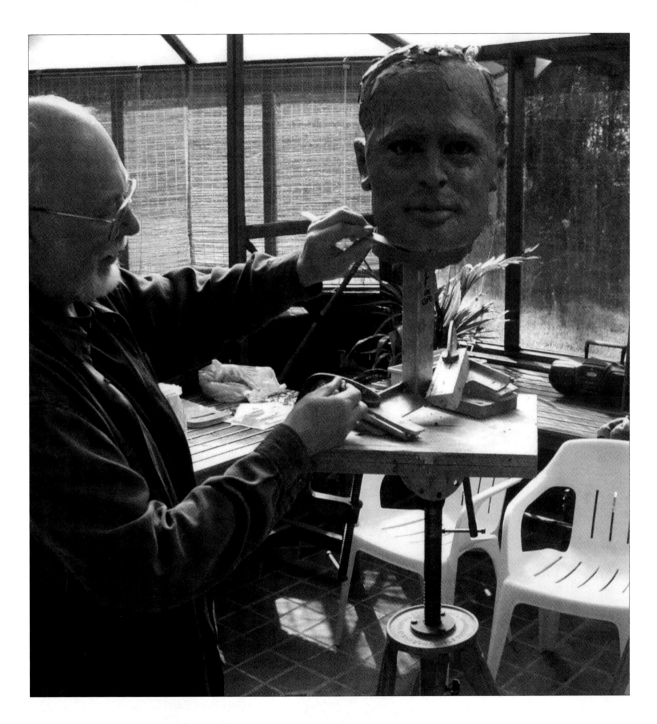

A statue of Sir Douglas Bader is something that many people have long considered appropriate. In 2000, Lord March, the owner of Goodwood Airfield & Motor Racing Circuit, decided that he wished to commemorate the site's association with this most famous of wartime aviators. Appropriately Kenneth Potts, a close friend of the author, was chosen to produce such a tribute. Dilip Sarkar produced all of the necessary historical and photographic references, from which Ken produced a stunning 3D image. At the time of writing, it is anticipated that the statue will be located adjacent to Goodwood's main entrance and unveiled on August 9th, 2001, the 60th anniversary of DB's last operational wartime flight. Ken is pictured in his studio working on the clay figure, which will ultimately be cast in bronze.

On February 2nd, 2000, Lady Bader received the OBE in recognition of her work for the disabled. Her Ladyship is pictured here at Buckingham Palace on that memorable occasion with her children, Jane Garrett, Michael Murray and Wendy McCleave.

The realities of earning an OBE and charity fund raising: Lady Bader Working 'in the field'.

And finally….. The young and old come together at the Douglas Bader Centre: amputees Harry Wells (left) and Callum Self. The incredibly positive impact of Douglas Bader's inspirational life is perfectly encapsulated in this photograph.

What the Celebrities Say

In his lifetime, Sir Douglas Bader played golf with other celebrities, many of whom remain household names today. During the preparation of this book, The Douglas Bader Foundation invited some of them to comment on their old friend and sporting opponent. These are reproduced below, and all make interesting reading with which to close this tribute.

Sir Sean Connery

I first met Douglas through our very good mutual friend, Sir Iain Stewart, when I was up in Glasgow directing a documentary on Fairfields Shipyard on the Clyde. Douglas was doing his never-ending work for amputees. My first impression of him was his stability, how very settled he was in his own skin and his tremendous enthusiasm. In time, I really appreciated his application and all his other qualities that golf reveals, both as a partner and as an opponent. He was tough and fair with great zest. His work was raising the profile and delivering the lack of facilities for amputees. His accomplishments in this field are second to none.

Another good friend of mine is David Murray, Chairman of Glasgow Rangers, a hugely successful entrepreneur. David had a terrible car crash hitting a tree, losing both of his legs. During his recovery, the first voice he was to hear was Douglas Bader explaining what David had to do, where he must go and why. He made the introductions and the arrangements. That was twenty five years ago and David Murray now has his own Trust for amputees. The Murray Foundation, of which I am proud to be a Trustee. Douglas I miss you.

Sir Henry Cooper OBE KSG

My lasting memory of Sir Douglas is of him stomping around the Hills of Gleneagles Golf Club playing in the Pro-Celebrity Golf on BBC.

It was a priviledge to be able to call him my friend.

Peter Allis

I first met Douglas Bader round about 1946/7, I was 15 or 16 years of age and had just played in the Boys' Championship at the Bruntsfield Golf Club on the west side of Edinburgh. I'd been beaten in the semi-final at the 19th hole and came home a little crestfallen having been made favourite to win the event by no less a figure than Leonard Crawley, the esteemed golf correspondent of the Daily Telegraph.

Within a few days of me arriving home, Douglas Bader arrived. He had met my father on numerous occasions and they had enjoyed an occasional round of golf. Father introduced me and told him of my recent golfing battles in Edinburgh. Somewhere along the line someone said, "Douglas has had a few battles too but more dangerous than going out of bounds or three putting!". We went out and played 9 holes and I marvelled at his ability to strike the ball and stride round the golf course in the most purposeful way. I can see him now, that tight, wavy hair, the little pipe stuck in the corner of his mouth, the twinkle in his eye, his enthusiasm and the way he called everybody "old boy" irrespective of age.

As the years went by we saw each other quite often and when the Pro-Celebrity Golf series began on BBC2 in 1974 it wasn't long before Douglas participated. In fact in 1982 he had a heart attack whilst playing out of the bunker in front of the 10th green on the Ailsa Course. He was about to play when suddenly he collapsed. People who knew Douglas didn't immediately rush to his aid because he hated anyone to fuss over him and you thought any minute he would jiggle himself into some

position or other and rise to his feet, he didn't. He was helped out of the bunker and taken back to the hotel. The doctor was called and we wondered what the outcome would be. We didn't have to wait long, about 7.30 that night he arrived full of bonhomie as if nothing had happened.

A remarkable man but perhaps a difficult one to work for because he could do most things better than anybody with two legs! He played golf to single figures, drove a car very well, flew aeroplanes, was a great raconteur and had a keen eye for business. I often wondered what it would be like to be in his employ!

I only saw him upstaged once and that was by Henry Cotton when the Bowmaker Tournament was played at The Berkshire Golf Club. It was a terribly wet day and everyone came in off the course absolutely sodden. Douglas was sitting in the locker room "removing his legs", the stumps wrapped in a soft, white blanket, but they looked red and sore. Cotton came in complaining about the weather, he went on and on! Douglas looked up and said "Good God man, I don't know what you're complaining about". (Incidentally, it was a cold-ish day and Douglas had gone round just wearing his familiar plus fours and a blue airtex short sleeved shirt). "Moan, moan, moan, are you afraid of a bit of rain?" To which Cotton uttered the immortal line "It's alright for you Douglas, your feet don't get wet". He lent back, roared with laughter and carried on. What a man.

Bruce Forsyth

Douglas was someone I had so much admiration for in so many ways. His courage was unequalled, his personality so engaging and his sense of humour so infectious. How he chose golf with his disability I will never know, a game where balance is so essential and co-ordination is imperative. But he did it and mastered it.

The last time I saw him was in Turnberry where we played a match for the BBC Pro Celebrity Golf television series. For one shot he had to climb into this very steep bunker and out again. He had played magnificently but this shot took so much out of him that shortly afterwards he didn't feel too good and they rushed him back to the hotel. We were all very worried about him but come dinnertime down he came, large as life as though he'd just walked out of a health farm .... but that was Douglas!

Seve Ballesteros

I recall the last time that I played golf with Douglas Bader in a Pro Celebrity tournament shortly before his death. It was obvious by the reception that he received from the spectators that he enjoyed enormous fame in the UK as a war hero, but I was always taken by surprise by his skill on the golf course.

For a man with no legs to have learned to play the game so well and use so effectively such a wide range of shots at first took me by surprise. But it was my privilege to soon get to know Sir Douglas and I am proud too, that we shared not just a love of the game, but a friendship. Once I got to know the man well and understand his very positive and uncompromising outlook on life as a whole, it came as no surprise that Douglas was an exceptional man who was determined to give a good account of himself no matter who he came against.

This he did in abundance in our last round together in Scotland during the summer of 1982. His company was a joy and I am honoured to have known and been friends with a man who showed so many so much.

Seve Ballesteros
May 2001

THE DOUGLAS BADER FOUNDATION
Charity Registration No 800435

We hope that you have enjoyed reading this book and, like so many in the past, are inspired by the story, courage and determination of a true hero amongst men, who took every obstacle that presented itself in his purposeful stride, albeit through necessity on occasions, rather ungainly!

You have read of how, today, The Douglas Bader Foundation strives to continue Douglas's inspirational work amongst the disabled community by providing support in the best way that it is able.

As Sir Douglas once said himself *"a disabled person who fights back is not handicapped………he is INSPIRED"*.

You can play a part in continuing the work that this unquestionably great man embarked upon so many years ago.

**Please help us to keep the "Bader Spirit" alive and
HELP US TO HELP THEM FIGHT BACK!**

Support our work by making a donation, deed of covenant, a bequest or legacy. Remember, every penny helps!

To contribute or for further information please contact:-

*Keith Delderfield, Director of Operations.
THE DOUGLAS BADER FOUNDATION
The Douglas Bader Centre, Roehampton Lane, London SW15 5DZ
Tel: 020 8788 1551   Fax: 020 8789 5622
e.mail douglasbaderfdn@btinternet.com*

or

*Administration Office, 45 Dundale Road, Tring, Herts HP23 5BU.
Tel/Fax: 01442 826662 Mobile: 07831 596015
e.mail keith.delderfield@btinternet.com*